Better Homes and Gardens®
3-INGREDIENT
decorating

3-Ingredient Decorating
Editor: Paula Marshall
Project Manager/Writer: Rebecca Jerdee
Graphic Designer: Sundie Ruppert
Copy Chief: Terri Fredrickson
Publishing Operations Manager: Karen Schirm
Book Production Managers: Pam Kvitne, Marjorie J. Schenkelberg, Rick von Holdt, Mark Weaver
Contributing Copy Editor: Jane Woychick
Contributing Proofreaders: Carol Boken, Lisa Baker, Becky Etchen
Contributing Photographers: Bill Hopkins, Greg Scheideman
Indexer: Kathleen Poole
Editorial Assistants: Kaye Chabot, Karen McFadden
Edit and Design Production Coordinator: Mary Lee Gavin

Meredith® Books
Editor in Chief: Linda Raglan Cunningham
Design Director: Matt Strelecki
Managing Editor: Gregory H. Kayko
Executive Editor: Denise L. Caringer

Publisher: James D. Blume
Executive Director, Marketing: Jeffrey Myers
Executive Director, New Business Development: Todd M. Davis
Executive Director, Sales: Ken Zagor
Director, Operations: George A. Susral
Director, Production: Douglas M. Johnston
Business Director: Jim Leonard

Vice President and General Manager: Douglas J. Guendel

Better Homes and Gardens® Magazine
Editor in Chief: Karol DeWulf Nickell
Deputy Editor, Home Design: Oma Blaise Ford

Meredith Publishing Group
President, Publishing Group: Stephen M. Lacy
Vice President-Publishing Director: Bob Mate

Meredith Corporation
Chairman and Chief Executive Officer: William T. Kerr

In Memoriam: E. T. Meredith III (1933-2003)

All of us at Meredith® Books are dedicated to providing you with information and ideas to enhance your home. We welcome your comments and suggestions. Write to us at: Meredith Books, Home Decorating and Design Editorial Department, 1716 Locust St., Des Moines, IA 50309-3023.

If you would like to purchase any of our home decorating and design, cooking, crafts, gardening, or home improvement books, check wherever quality books are sold. Or visit us at: bhgbooks.com
Cover Photograph: Bill Hopkins

a simple plan

An easy cake recipe that gets you rave reviews every time you use it—that's a thrill. Pulling together a beautiful room with a few mainstays will give you an even bigger kick. This book of room recipes shows you how to get amazing results with only three key ingredients: background, furniture, and accessories. Turn the next few pages to see how three-ingredient decorating can give you the power and confidence to fill your home with style, function, and beauty—and the thrill of it all.

GETTING STARTED

A bright, exotic mood steps into this space with purple walls, orange woodwork, a bowl of light, and shiny laminate flooring.

BACKGROUND

WALLS paint; glaze; paneling; wallpaper; mirrors

FLOORS wood; tile; carpet; paint; rugs

ARCHITECTURAL FEATURES embellished with wood or faux-painted moldings; stained; painted

FIXED LIGHTING ceiling fixtures; recessed lighting; chandeliers; sconces; swing-arm lamps

FIXED FURNITURE shelves; cupboards; cabinetry; sinks; counters; sanitary fixtures

WINDOW COVERINGS fabric panels; shutters; shades

ROOM DIVIDERS screens; curtains

To stir up some style, begin with the base: background. Think of background as a stage backdrop, a mood-setter, the basic shell or envelope that wraps around the living that goes on inside a room. A good backdrop will speak up, blend into the conversation, and express the tone and attitude that tells your story—or at least the chapter of the story that takes place in that particular space. If your floors, walls, ceilings, architecture, lighting, and fixed cabinetry seem bland, grab a paintbrush, step up to the plate, and get in the decorating game.

Clear the decks. If possible, empty a room and start your decorating recipe from scratch. Even if you plan on using furniture or accessories you already have, it's refreshing to remove them for a time and let the room be purely a space. Clearing out gives you a chance to de-clutter, re-organize possessions, and find new uses and places for old standbys. Beyond that, it's a marvelous way to give yourself plenty of elbowroom for brandishing that paintbrush.

When it's all about talk, talk, talk, walls that make room for words bring communication into the foreground.

Although the materials are inexpensive, velvet curtains and mirrored walls, as shown on page 36, give a room the look of luxury and glamour.

An accent strip, positioned between two soft greens, wakes up sleepy walls.

Light, airy colors and soft textures set the stage for quiet relaxation after-hours.

A room-dividing curtain sets off a small area in a multitasking space, reserving it for a special function.

Sometimes a quiet backdrop is best. This one graciously falls back to let attention focus on other decorating ingredients still to come.

1

What's a table without something to hold? An accessory display waiting to happen.

Furniture

SEATING upholstered sofas and chairs; occasional chairs; dining chairs; folding chairs; benches; stools; settees

TABLES coffee; dining; bedside; occasional; kitchen islands; counters; desks

BEDS mattress and box spring; four-poster/wood-frame; sleeper sofas; cribs; cradles; futons; built-ins

STORAGE cabinets; cupboards; chests of drawers; bookcases; carts; armoires; trunks; boxes

Furniture plays multiple roles on your decorating stage. It must be in the right place at the right time, offer comfort and convenience wherever and whenever you need it, and wisely store items you want to keep on hand. Think of furniture as the central ingredient in a room, the link that binds together the background and accessories in your decorating recipe. Furniture brings congeniality to a room; each piece is like a thoughtful host, offering a place to sit, a surface to set things on, or a pleasant focal point.

Fit Furniture to Function in your spaces. In a house occupied by one or two people, three pieces—a bed, a sofa, and a table—form the core of the furniture collection. Once you have places to eat, sleep, and sit, add such embellishments as secondary tables, chairs, storage, and entertainment pieces. Well-chosen pieces will allow you to comfortably read, work, talk, play, gather friends, entertain, and feel relaxed and at peace. Choose your furniture carefully, buying first for comfort and second for style. Keep your furniture style consistent to ensure a cohesive look that expresses your personality.

With a little staging, furniture can pretend to be anything it likes. Here, two bar-height chairs pull up to a coffeehouse counter—at home in a suburban kitchen.

Even the most basic bed—a mattress, boxspring, and standard metal frame—can invite sleep and dreams.

2

Ask an armoire to do double duty. Besides functioning as an entertainment center, this one blends with a bamboo screen to separate the living room from the entry.

Too many legs can spoil the look. Add a tablecloth for a measure of modesty.

Where floor space is limited, stackable storage fits the bill.

Like the people who will occupy them, chairs gather sociably around a coffee table. Side tables stand by, ready to serve.

Bookmarks collected from museum stores let you display fragments of great paintings you saw while on tour.

accessories

LIGHTING task; accent; ambient; candles; lantern

PERSONAL COMFORTS pillows; linens; towels; throws; quilts; blankets; bedcovers

CONVENIENCES mirrors; cookware; tableware; clocks; vases; fireplace tools; planters; candleholders; trays

NATURAL TOUCHES green plants; cut flowers; fruit; woven baskets; gourds; terraria; fish tanks; birdcages

ARTS & ENTERTAINMENT artwork; books and magazines; DVD and CD collections; arts and crafts collections; electronics; travel souvenirs; antiques; sports equipment; architectural salvage; photographs

Blending in accessories—the third ingredient of your decorating recipe—is like decorating a cake or propping a stage for a theater production. Without frosting, a cake seems less festive; without accessories, a room lacks the spark of personality. Accessories—functional and not-so-functional objects of beauty—bring a room to life. A lovely lamp and a stack of books set on a chairside table invite an armchair traveler to explore by reading. A fragrant lavender-filled pillow coaxes a weary soul to sleep, and a DVD rack offers instant escape.

Know when to stop. Adding too many accessories is like spoiling the soup with too much seasoning. In general, accessorize "to taste" and follow your instincts, sprinkling in what feels right for you and the way you live. If you desire simplicity, you're a discriminating soul and only a distinguished few accessories will enter your rooms. If you desire close company and coziness, you will be inclined to accessorize more. Watch for accessorizing ideas in the photographs and room recipes throughout this book.

Create the ambience of a coffee shop right in your kitchen with a display of your favorite coffee beans and cups.

Soften your life with cushions and comforts. Accessorizing with textures adds visual interest and encourages hand-on use of a room.

Give yourself a reading rack that's within easy reach. Let appealing magazine covers "hang around" as affordable art.

3

Entertain with a wardrobe of table linens and belt your napkins with fashionable rings. Let your table settings shine by candlelight.

Light your face in the morning with a strip o lights over your bathroom mirror. It's stylish and practical in any bath setting.

Collect beautiful objects purely because you love having them around. You could say their function is to please you.

entrances

When guests cross your threshold, does your entry welcome them? Does it reflect the rooms beyond? If it's only a passageway, coax it into something more. The first part of this chapter shows you how to create an entry where none exists. The rest of the chapter offers decorating makeovers for a variety of entrances. An entry is the gateway to your home, so make it as welcoming as you are and jazz it up with paint, light, and creativity. Turn the pages to learn how.

Guests can't wait to see the next act once they step into the drama of this exotic entry. Here's a recipe that carves out an entry from living space and lifts the lid on color and decorative treasures.

JEWEL BOX

 1 BACKGROUND

WALL AND TRIM COLORS orange; lavender

ROOM DIVIDER bamboo screen; back of living room armoire

FLOOR COVERINGS hardwood flooring; stripe wool runner

FIXED LIGHTING wall sconce

 2 FURNITURE

SEATING black and tan cane chair

CONVENIENT CATCHALL SURFACES console; top of small chest

STORAGE small chest

 3 ACCESSORIES

MOOD LIGHTING candles

CONVENIENCES mirror; tray for keys and mail

WELCOMING TOUCHES plants; pillows; conversation-starting objects of interest; art; pottery; clip rings

Wood trim color matches the accent wall along the side of the entry, giving the room a colorful wrap.

1

A bowl of light matches the sconce in the main living space adjacent to the entrance.

A scintillating lavender paint that's not too purple, pink, or blue creates an exotic backdrop.

A wool runner draws a path, directing those who come and go.

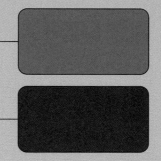

WALLS To make a room into a color box like this one, examine the paint strips at paint stores. Select two colors that have about the same intensity (brightness) and value (lightness or darkness). Adding more colors can result in chaos. A partnership of two hues with values and intensities in common keeps the design in control.

BACKGROUND Like the velvet lining of a jewelry box, these painted walls suggest the rich vibes of faraway places and mysterious objects. This entry is part of the main living space (see the first living room featured in the chapter on living rooms on page 34), so its color palette matches the main room.

To paint the room, mask off the edges of the door frame, baseboard, and crown moldings with painter's tape. Paint the main wall of the entire space (including the living space beyond) with the midvalue lavender color; paint the opposite wall lavender as well. The ends of the room act as accent walls, so cover them using a deep orange interior latex paint with an eggshell finish. Paint all woodwork trims in the same deep orange color, but use a semigloss latex enamel for durability.

Hang a sconce to light the entry end of the room; this creates continuity with the lines of the sconces in the living room. With their beams directed upward, sconces are useful for general lighting of a large space. Other light sources provide different effects. For example, a table lamp lights a small surface for reading or other tasks; candlelight adds drama, intimacy, and a festive mood.

Lay a runner over hardwood flooring to direct traffic through the space. This wool runner with quiet stripes is barely noticeable, but it effectively softens the overall look of the entry.

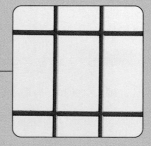

WINDOWS Consider the front door as a design element that can stand alone. Frosted glass in a front door is one option for letting in as much light as possible without losing privacy. To frost your own glass, tape ½-inch-wide painter's tape inside the edges of the mullions. Frost the open areas with etching cream (available at crafts supply stores). Remove the tape to reveal a faux beveled edge around each pane.

FLOOR COVERINGS Anything goes for a runner on dark, neutral flooring. Instead of laying down another neutral, such as the rug, *opposite,* consider using a more colorful kilim runner that repeats the design motifs you choose for the wall art or table displays.

F u r n i t u r e Without furniture, an entry remains merely a passageway. Add comfort with such functional pieces as a bench, small chairs, or a console table to hold keys, packages, or collections. If your front door opens right into your living room as this one does, create an entryway by making a visual barrier perpendicular to the door. Here, the entertainment armoire in the living room backs up against an imaginary line drawn for an entry wall, creating a half-wall between the two spaces. The floor screen continues the line begun by the armoire, closing off the space. Across the way, a console table balances the space and awaits a display of art objects similar to those in the living space.

To find furniture pieces for a fascinating entry with import appeal, shop with a floor plan of your space drawn on paper. Also carry a tape measure to determine whether a piece of furniture you discover fits the space. Decide on a primary focus—Asian, Indian, African, Balinese, or Caribbean—and look for pieces with lines and details indigenous to that country or continent. However, it's fine to toss in something from a different distant land—every good room recipe is seasoned with a mix of influences. To maintain unity among a group of disparate pieces, keep all of them within the same color palette.

This long, narrow table can display a collection of art objects. A lower shelf, built into the table, provides an additional surface for storage.

A chair provides seating for removing or putting on footwear.

Food for thought...

Explore import stores for foreign-made furniture to season an exotic decorating plan. Some stores import ready-to-assemble benches, chairs, settees, and tables that are sold in flat packs. Judge how a piece will look and fit in your space by viewing the assembled samples on display. Note what country the furniture pieces come from for clues to the origins of the designs. Also check out furniture possibilities on the Internet.

A floor screen cuts away space from the living room, creating an entry.

2

A small cabinet offers storage and a surface for keys or mail. It also hides most of the back of the living room armoire.

Fruit and flowers on a console welcome guests.

A mirror hides the upper back of an armoire that faces the living area.

3

A string of museum bookmarks reflects a homeowner's love of art. The mini masterpieces invite conversation and lingering.

accessories If art, collections, or plants are part of your household, introduce them in the entry. As objects that attract attention, they slow the dash through an entrance, letting you meet and greet guests in a leisurely fashion. Visitors will be inclined to pause and linger for a look around the space.

Fruit and flowers are the best way to freshen an entry before guests arrive. Natural objects offer the eye something familiar and timeless. They carry no hint of man-made influences; they merely extend beautiful colors, shapes, and textures that everyone appreciates. Fresh fruit and flowers in the entry tell your friends that they are special enough for you to go to an extra decorating effort to greet them. As William Shakespeare wrote, "One touch of nature makes the whole world kin."

Mirrors, candles, and trays. Mirrors visually enlarge entries. They also allow last-minute primping before you leave the house. In the arrangement for this entry, the mirror has another purpose: It hides the back of an entertainment armoire, a piece used to create a dividing wall between the entry and the living area. Candles set in front of the mirror create sparkle and add drama for special occasions. Set a tray on an entryway cabinet as a key and mail catchall.

Wire display rack. A minimalist device for displaying favorite pictures, snapshots, and postcards, this type of rack is popular for entry displays. Here, the rack displays print images hung from metal clips that are strung on the wires. Items on display can be easily changed. To make the rack, purchase four screw eyes,

four small eye/hook turnbuckles, and a couple of packages of #6 galvanized mirror cord. For a secure display, locate two wall studs and fasten the screw eyes along the studs. Set two pairs of screw eyes for two lines of wire, using a tape measure and a level to ensure that the wires hang straight. Space the two lines about 8 inches apart. Thread the clips onto the two wires and fasten the eyes of the turnbuckles to the ends of the wires. Place the hook ends of the turnbuckles through the screw eyes and turn the screws in the turnbuckles until the wires are tense enough to hang pictures.

In this display, a walking stick creates a vertical line, balancing the horizontal lines of the wires and console.

For elegant simplicity and tranquillity in an entry, decorate with pairs. The rhythm and order of pairs please guests and residents alike.

TWO'S COMPANY

1 — B a c k g r o u n d

WALL AND TRIM COLOR white

FLOOR COVERING hardwood

FIXED LIGHTING overhead recessed lighting

2 — F u r n i t u r e

SEATING two matched chairs

CONVENIENT CATCHALL SURFACE round side table

3 — a c c e s s o r i e s

MOOD LIGHTING table lamp

PERSONAL TOUCHES a pair of prints; a sign; a group of three small objects; a white vase

WELCOMING TOUCH fresh flowers

Paint a white backdrop gallery wall in your entry to set off a display of your personal art collection. The artwork will reflect your personality and let guests know what decorative style they can expect around the next corner. Paint the trim in a semi-gloss that matches the wall color.

Paint a pair of curvy chairs with white paint. Before the paint dries, wipe some of it off the surfaces and edges to give the chairs an old-world look. Upholster the seats with matching fabric. Many chairs, such as these dining chairs, have seats you can remove with a screwdriver. Ask a friend to help you stretch your chosen fabric over the chair pads; then staple the edges to the undersides of the seats. To begin the symmetrical arrangement, choose a centerline (axis) for the design. Center the side table on this imaginary line. Park the chairs on either side of the table.

Arrange art symmetrically. Place a table lamp on the center of the table toward the back to emphasize the central axis of the arrangement. Hang two same-size, similar-subject prints with matching frames and hangers, positioning one print directly above each chair. Without hanging the prints too high, leave a comfortable breathing space between them and the tops of the chairs. Ideally the images will be at eye level for a standing guest. Hang a horizontal sign directly centered on the lamp to cap off the arrangement. To take some of the stiffness out of the symmetrical design, add asymmetry by placing a group of three objects on one side of the table. Choose objects whose visual weight and shape balance the vase of fresh flowers you put on the other side of the table.

Crisp white walls create a gallery-style space for a personal collection of furniture and art.

PARIS

A table light makes a space feel more intimate.

A pair of chairs brings symmetry, order, and a touch of formality to an entry.

Inexpensive painted 1×3s molding, mounted 63 inches from the floor, anchors the soaring ceiling and draws the eye up the stairs.

An uncovered sidelight lets in light and allows view of anyone knocking at the door.

Stretch limited space with useful items. Coat hooks screwed directly into the molding keep outdoor wear out of the way.

The small, awkward white space of a standard grade split foyer often goes untouched for lack of decorating ideas. Here's an inviting solution.

warm welcome

 1 BACKGROUND

WALL TREATMENT white paint; brown grass-cloth

FLOOR COVERINGS hardwood; stairway carpeting

 2 Furniture

SEATING white ladder-back chair

 3 accessories

STORAGE wall hooks

CONVENIENCES toss rug; mirror hung from hook

Create a textural backdrop with a reedy grass-cloth wallcovering that makes the space feel more intimate. Applied as a wainscot, it introduces a horizontal element that balances the dramatic vertical space. You'll need vinyl wallcovering paste and a brush for applying adhesive to the backs of the grass-cloth panels. On the wall, mark a horizontal line 63 inches from the floor, where the tops of the panels will reach. Continue the line at an angle up the stairs. Measure and cut panels to fit the walls, starting with the first panel at the corner by the door. Working on a wide table surface, brush vinyl paste onto the back of the first panel. Start at the line marked on the wall and gently press the panel to the wall with your hands. With a level, check to see if the edge of the panel is plumb. Continue adding panels until the wainscot is complete, butting the edge of each panel against the next one (the butted seam will be visible and is part of the grass-cloth look). Cut 1×3-inch boards to top off the grass-cloth wainscot. Paint the boards white before attaching them to the walls with screws at stud locations.

Set a chair in the only available space near the door. It offers all comers a chance to sit down and take off muddy boots before stepping up the carpeted staircase.

Stretch limited space with useful accessories. Hang coat hooks by screwing them directly into the molding. String a mirror on ribbon and hang it on one of the hooks. Toss a rug on the floor to catch dirt or sand brought in on the bottoms of shoes.

If the entryway into your home is little more than a narrow passage, give it a makeover that takes up minimal space but conjures up much more presence and spirit.

practical magic

 B a c k g r o u n d

WALLS, DOOR wainscot; lattice trims; wide base moldings

PAINT COLORS pale yellow; light khaki; wheat; white

FLOOR COVERING wood laminate

FIXED LIGHTING paper shade

 F u r n i t u r e

SEATING small folding chairs doubling as catchall surfaces

STORAGE coat closet on opposite wall

 a c c e s s o r i e s

PERSONAL TOUCHES antique letters; antique fishing poles

Build a wainscot using plywood panels. The purpose of this wainscot is fourfold: As a decorating tool, it makes the narrow entrance appear wider and more stylish. As a practical prop, it muffles sound and hides dented walls, protecting them against further hard knocks from daily traffic. To make the wainscot, remove base moldings from the existing walls. From 1-inch-thick plywood, cut 35-inch-high wainscot panels to fit the lengths of the walls. Using a stud sensor, locate wall studs, then nail the plywood panels to the walls at the stud locations for a secure hold. Paint the walls above the wainscot pale yellow. Paint the wainscot light khaki. Paint the hollow-core door with the same colors, making a 6-inch border in yellow around a khaki center. For wainscot trims, cut 1×6-inch boards for base moldings, enough lattice battens to apply every 12 inches, and a 1×1½-inch rail to top the wainscot. To trim the door, miter a frame of lattice to surround the khaki center. Prime and paint all trims white. When the trims are dry, nail the base moldings over the wainscot at the bottom, fasten the lattice strips over the face of the plywood wainscot, and top the wainscot with the rail. Glue and nail the white frame on the face of the door around the khaki center.

Keep furniture sparse in a narrow entrance. A small seat is sufficient in an entrance with a coat closet. These antique golf chairs look good and take up little space.

Arrange antique letters on the wainscot rail molding—a perfect ledge for the slim flea market find. Hang a paper shade on a ceiling fixture that warms the space and lights the way.

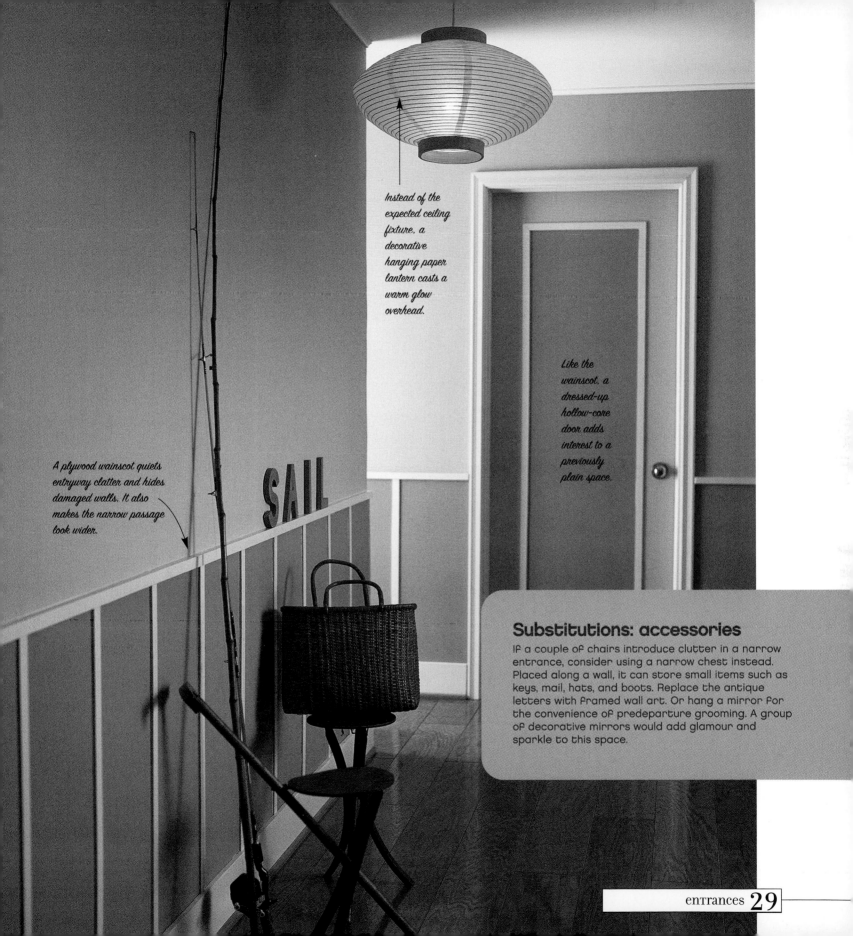

Instead of the expected ceiling fixture, a decorative hanging paper lantern casts a warm glow overhead.

Like the wainscot, a dressed-up hollow-core door adds interest to a previously plain space.

A plywood wainscot quiets entryway clutter and hides damaged walls. It also makes the narrow passage look wider.

SAIL

Substitutions: accessories

If a couple of chairs introduce clutter in a narrow entrance, consider using a narrow chest instead. Placed along a wall, it can store small items such as keys, mail, hats, and boots. Replace the antique letters with framed wall art. Or hang a mirror for the convenience of predeparture grooming. A group of decorative mirrors would add glamour and sparkle to this space.

Whitewashed rough cedar paneling makes a clean, textured backdrop for a display of collectibles.

Rounded shapes in the entry allow two different chairs to coexist with a reproduction mirror.

Food for thought...

Look for interesting, one-of-a-kind objects that can be made into table lamps at a lamp shop. Use decorative mounting and attach a base when it's impractical to drill holes for wiring. Dress up a shade with hand-sewn or hot-glued trims (beaded trim is a fashionable look). Collect painted metal tole trays, plates, old leather books, boxes, baskets, and unframed paintings and use them to create backdrops and elevations. For an extra display dimension, watch for salvaged wall brackets and fragments on your antiquing expeditions.

French doors open onto a preview of interesting collectibles. An overscale mirror anchors the diverse grouping in this entry.

open sesame

 1 BACKGROUND

WALL COLOR white

DOOR AND TRIM COLOR white

FLOOR COVERING ceramic tile in 12-inch squares

FIXED LIGHTING antique glass chandelier

 2 FURNITURE

SEATING Louis XVI-style straight chair; tufted Edwardian-style English chair

STORAGE/SURFACE demilune (half-round) table

 3 accessories

MOOD LIGHTING table lamp

CONVENIENCES mirror; tray

PERSONAL TOUCHES books; boxes; baskets; prints; plates

WELCOMING TOUCH fresh flowers in a silver vase

Cover the entrance walls with rough cedar paneling. For added texture and a clean backdrop for displaying collectibles, paint the paneling with white semigloss paint. Paint wood trim and window and door frames in the same white. Lay an area rug—antique or reproduction—over a tile floor. Replace a standard ceiling fixture with a charming antique chandelier that fits your collecting style.

Gather furniture. Look for an overscale mirror to set the tone for the entrance decor. Keep your eyes open for chair possibilities. Lone chairs that have strayed from a set are good buys. Shop for shape and construction; finish and fabric can always be changed. A well-made secondhand chair is a better long-term investment than a cheap new one. A matching pair of chairs ensures an easy arrangement, but it's more interesting to work with two loners. Buy a pair of odd chairs that have lines in common. The rounded lines of the two chairs, *opposite,* make them a compatible pair.

Arrange collectibles on and around the furniture grouping. Group cultures and continents for harmony. For example, delicate Asian accessories, such as a Japanese Imari plate and a Chinese mud-man figure, mix easily with the rich colors of leather-bound books and the refinement of blue and white Chinese export porcelain. Use books and wooden boxes to elevate smaller items. This will give them greater stature, and balance the arrangement overall. Remember that pairs of objects, such as the fern prints and green plates, *opposite,* calm a diverse display.

LIVING
rooms

A well-designed living room lives and entertains the way you do. Whether your design style is formal or casual, sparse or over-the-top, take a thoughtful look at the design elements and layout in your living room. Are they in sync with the way you live? If not, peruse the pages of this chapter for ways to cook up more life, style, and function for the most versatile space in your home. The first part of this chapter reveals the other side of the entry featured on pages 16-23. The rest of the chapter serves up other ideas for living room decor.

Deep colors and sumptuous textures beckon from this inviting room. A soft mix of fabrics—silk, chenille, velvet, and taffeta—combines with a spicy blend of modern and ethnic furnishings. Turn the pages to see how the ingredients come together.

velvet allure

1 BACKGROUND

WALL AND TRIM COLORS orange; lavender

WINDOW COVERINGS AND ROOM DIVIDER velvet panels; framed mirror panels; bamboo screen

FLOOR COVERINGS hardwood flooring; wool carpet inset

2 FURNITURE

SEATING scarlet sectional sofa; black and tan cane chair

TABLES glass nesting tables; wood nesting tables

STORAGE wall-hung shelf unit; entertainment armoire

3 accessories

MOOD LIGHTING beaded floor lamp; wall sconces

PERSONAL COMFORTS silk pillows; throw

EYE CANDY fruit and flowers; vase; glassware; handcrafted collectibles; beaded pillow; platters

1

Mirror tiles, attached to the wall, artificially extend the window and add glamour to the space. They also double the light factor in the room.

Trim color matches the accent walls at the ends of the room. The sultry orange plays against velvety lavender hues on the main wall.

A wool carpet, inset in hardwood flooring, defines the space for the island of furniture to come.

BACKGROUND A number of surface textures—paint, glass, velvet, wool, wood, and mirror—create a rich lining for this boxlike room. The wall sconces next to the mirror panels match the sconce in the entry (page 17) and contribute symmetry.

To make the mirror panels, purchase 12-inch squares of mirror tile with self-adhesive backs. The panels shown here consist of 12 mirror tiles each. Measure your window to see how many mirror tiles you'll need to match its height. On each side of the window, find the halfway point from top to bottom; this is the starting point for setting the first tile. Following the gluing instructions that come with the tile, adhere 12 of the tiles along the side of one window in two vertical rows; repeat along the other window. When the mirror panels are in place, frame them in 2-inch-wide framing material painted to match the window frame.

To inset a piece of carpet inside a rim of do-it-yourself hardwood flooring, purchase carpet yardage of the desired size and enough do-it-yourself grooved planking to complete the remaining surface of the floor. Lay the carpet on the floor. Measure and cut the wood flooring to fit around the carpet. Lay the flooring. Cut the frame from 1-inch-thick lumber, rabbeting the inside edges to accommodate the height of the carpet. Attach the frame to the subflooring, pinning it in place with long nails.

Note: You can achieve the same effect by laying a piece of carpet over an existing floor and framing the carpet in wood that matched the floor color.

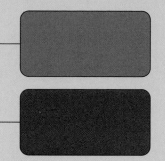
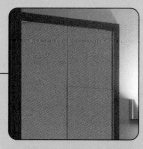

WALLS When creating a living/entry room, use the same colors in both spaces. See page 19 for advice on choosing colors. Paint the walls, window frames, baseboards, and crown moldings.

WINDOWS Expand the look and size of an existing window with panels of mirror tile on each side. The panels have the look of glass and mullioned windowpanes but are much easier to install than additional windows. Leave the mirror panels uncovered but add two velvet tab-top panels on a modern metal curtain rod over the window for privacy and softness. The panels also add another shade of lavender to the color scheme of the room.

FLOOR COVERINGS Purchase a carpet and do-it-yourself wood laminate from a flooring gallery. To inset a carpet, buy unbound low-pile carpet and enough wood flooring to surround it. To lay a piece of carpet over a wall-to-wall wood floor—as if it were an area rug instead of an inset carpet—buy a piece of carpet and ask to have it bound.

FurnITure Here's the other side of the decorating story begun on page 16. On the flip side of the entry, the furniture used to create the dividing line serves the living room. Display shelves, side tables, and upholstered seating pieces are moved into the living space.

To make the shelf unit, cut 12-inch-deep shelves from medium-density fiberboard. You'll need two 8-foot-long pieces and one 6-foot-long piece for the shelves. For dividers, cut five 12×12 and four 12×15-inch pieces. To assemble, rout slots in the shelves to accept the dividers at the ends and at equal intervals along the length of each piece (the unit has four equal 12-inch-high compartments on the top tier and three equal 15-inch-high compartments on the bottom one). Center the shorter, bottom tier under the top tier. Glue and nail the dividers into the routed slots. Paint the wall unit to match the orange trim color of the moldings.

To arrange the furniture, *opposite*, hang the shelf unit so that the top shelf is 38 inches above the floor. Install the corner unit of the sectional sofa far enough away from the main wall to allow draperies to flow naturally and far enough away from the shelf unit to allow for adequate access. Set the single seating pieces along the line established by the corner unit, spacing them at least 12 to 15 inches apart to allow for quick access to the shelf unit. Expand the seating group by placing another corner unit opposite the first one and attaching a two seat sectional to the open end of each unit. Add an ottoman to the end of one two-seat sectional to complete the U-shape arrangement. Place the glass nesting tables in the center of the furniture island; add the wood nesting tables beside the cane chair and at the end of the second two-seat sectional.

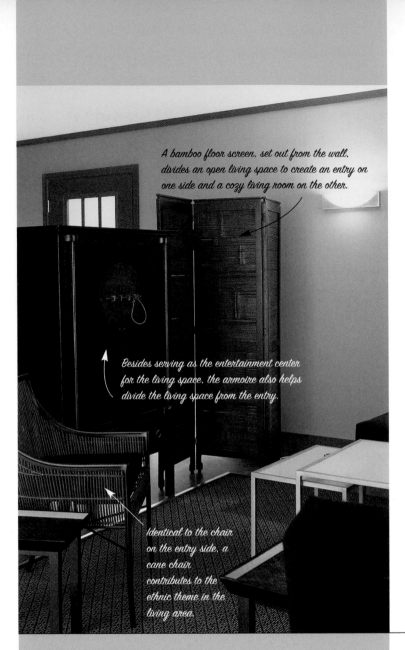

A bamboo floor screen, set out from the wall, divides an open living space to create an entry on one side and a cozy living room on the other.

Besides serving as the entertainment center for the living space, the armoire also helps divide the living space from the entry.

Identical to the chair on the entry side, a cane chair contributes to the ethnic theme in the living area.

Food for thought...

Let furniture tell your story. For example, create a formal look with antiques and reproductions featuring classic details: camelbacks on sofas, cabriole legs, ball-and-claw feet, or shield or lyre-shape chair backs. To make a formal but modern statement, combine 20th-century classics such as Barcelona and Wassily chairs. If your story is more casual, use oversize rolled-arm sofas with squashy cushions to set the mood.

A wall unit hangs inside space created by a bump-out wall. It's useful for storing books and collectibles and serves as a bar during parties.

Soft, plush seating covered in a soft mohair fabric assembles in a cozy U-shape configuration on the carpet.

2

Two sets of modern nesting tables easily expand or contract, depending on the entertainment needs of the moment.

Wooden nesting tables stand next to seating pieces for service. They also lend flavor to the ethnic part of this room recipe.

Embroidered and beaded fabrics and lush silk damask add more texture to the mohair-covered sectional.

A taste of the African landscape, dyed and carved gourds, settle into a large glass bowl to give guests something to talk about.

3

A reading ladder keeps favorite magazines and newspapers handy. The idea is borrowed from the racks used in public libraries and bookstore reading corners.

The mirror tiles on the wall reflect accessories placed around the room, giving them double exposure as eye candy.

a c c e s s o r i e s A room filled with beautiful, comfortable furniture needs one final ingredient to make it complete: personal accessories. To season a living room such as this, arrange small items that relax and comfort the body, and entertain the mind and soul. Select pieces that relate to each other and to the furniture pieces in the room. Use a theme—African and Asian handcrafts, for example—to help you assemble a collection of pieces that has colors and textures in common. Such objects offer earthy, ancient counterpoints to the slick, modern vibes of the main furniture pieces.

Layer pillows and throws in places where they'll be felt, used, and appreciated. End the length of the long sectional with a pair of artful pillows to delight the eye. Add another set of pillows on the pair of single seats to balance the look and provide cushiony comfort.

Arrange collectibles by balancing their weight values around the room. A symmetrical arrangement soothes the eye but lapses into boredom unless countered by an off-center item. For example, the matching wedding baskets displayed on matching stools on the shelf unit (see page 35) bring peace and order to the room. A large bowl on the coffee table balances the weight of the gourds and piques curiosity. For another example, a Chinese silk throw, loosely tossed over the back of the sofa, breaks up the tedious length of the sectional.

To make the reading ladder, you'll need two 5-foot-long 2×2s (for the sides) and six 16-inch-long, ⅜-inch-diameter wood dowels (for the rungs). To establish the rung placement, mark one ladder side at 3, 14, 26, 38, and 44 inches, measuring from the top end. Align the two lengths side-by-side in a vise with the first marked side facing up; precisely duplicate the rung marks on the second length. With the sides still clamped together, use a drill press to drill dowel holes 1 inch deep at the marks. Sand wood surfaces. Dry fit dowels (install without glue) to check for fit; sand and refit where necessary. When the dowels fit correctly, glue the rungs in place. Lay the rack flat for a day until the glue has dried. Paint the rack to match the color of the living room window frame.

An island cottage worth its sea salt needs a little bit of sass mingled with loads of sophistication. Ever-adaptable white gives this living room both.

sand castle

 1 B a c k g r o u n d

WALL AND TRIM COLOR white

WINDOW COVERINGS white shades for privacy

FLOOR COVERINGS light wood flooring; sisal rug

FIXED LIGHTING modern cable pendants

 2 F u r n i t u r e

SEATING upholstered chairs; shield-back chairs

TABLES round coffee table; side tables

 3 a c c e s s o r i e s

MOOD LIGHTING candles in fireplace; wall sconces

PERSONAL COMFORTS lacy shawl throw; cushions

EYE CANDY mantel bits and pieces; coffee table pieces; plants; mantel art

Paint walls, ceiling, and woodwork bright white. Using white satisfies the impulse for simple luxury and reflects natural light that streams through uncovered windows during the day (hanging white pleated shades or white blinds at the tops of the windows provides privacy in the evening). A large sisal area rug over the wood flooring defines the seating area and becomes the foundation for the layered white and sand color textures in the room.

Arrange two pairs of chairs, covered in variations of white, around a centrally located coffee table. Subtle colors and quiet patterns—a sand and white leaf design on the upholstered chairs and champagne and white stripes on two shield-back chairs—keep the room calm. For a coffee table, cut down the legs of a classic, secondhand dining table and paint it high-gloss white. Or purchase a new round coffee table with a smooth, glossy white finish. Place an iron plant table near a window and put an ottoman near a chair to serve as a footrest or tray stand.

Furnish flat surfaces with conveniences, comforts, and beautiful objects to bewitch the senses. For example, the coffee table offers small books between corbel bookends, daisies make bright faces in a clear glass, and fruit engages the appetite. Set green plants at intervals around the room and light large pillar candles in the firebox for ambience that soothes and delights.

Substitutions: seasonal changes

White is never limiting, and with accent changes, it can seem totally new each season. When falling temperatures and snowflakes make cocooning indoors so appealing, a few accent changes can warm body and soul. For example, iron masks of the North Wind and pedestal pots of winterberries could accent the mantel. On the coffee table, set a wide glass bowl filled with clear glass fishing floats. Garnish the glass globes with a string of white, battery-operated miniature lights.

Summertime sass appears as mantel art. Black and white tones bring verve and vitality to elegant white spaces filled with classic furniture.

Textures—iron, glass, even tufts of sea grass in a vase—add a bit of contrast or visual interest, but not enough to spoil the mood.

Geometric art, painted directly on the wall, adds a modern component to a traditional room.

Supporting-role taupe walls, neutral furnishings, and crisp white woodwork graciously let the wall art take center stage in this living room play.

Blue pillows and curtains repeat the accent color of the wall art at pleasing intervals.

For a quick circle stencil, use vinyl film from a crafts store. The film cuts cleanly with a crafts knife and has an adhesive back. Press the stencil to the wall, paint, and peel off.

Three bold blue and white color blocks, with the look of framed modern art, dress up a mantel and set the stage for the rest of the room.

squared away

1 BACKGROUND

WALL COLORS taupe walls; white woodwork; blue and white color-block wall art

WINDOW COVERINGS blue cotton tab-top panels

FLOOR COVERINGS wood laminate; bound sisal rug

FIXED LIGHTING overhead ceiling fixture

2 Furniture

SEATING taupe upholstered chair and ottoman

TABLES walnut side tables

3 accessories

MOOD LIGHTING table lamps

PERSONAL COMFORTS blue and white pillows; dark taupe chenille throw

EYE CANDY fire screen; silver vases; flowers; photo

Paint walls in a pale taupe color; paint all trim (base and crown moldings, fireplace surround) white. To paint the mantel/wall art, measure to the center of the mantel. Using a level and a colored pencil, draw three level squares centered and evenly spaced above the mantel. These 16-inch squares are 8 inches above the mantel and spaced 2 inches apart. Tape off each square. Paint each end square white and the middle square blue; remove tape and let the paint dry. With a level and a colored pencil, draw a square within each end square, leaving a 2-inch border. Tape off the inner square and paint blue using a paint roller (see photo, *opposite, above left*). Use a compass or dinner plate to draw a circle on cardboard or vinyl film; cut out. Use the cutout as a stencil to draw a circle in the middle square, leaving a 2-inch border at sides, top, and bottom. Paint the circle white; let dry. Wash the colored pencil lines away with a sponge and dishwashing detergent or shampoo. Touch up edges, if necessary. Hang blue tab-top curtains on plain modern rods. Place an area rug in front of the fireplace.

Arrange upholstered pieces around the fireplace and area rug. Place a sofa directly opposite the fireplace. Place side tables within arm's length near the seating pieces. (A classic seating arrangement includes a pair of armchairs that face each other at the ends of the sofa and two end tables that fill in the corners between chairs and sofa.)

For the final ingredient, choose accent pillows that repeat the square color-block theme set by the mantel art. Add a soft throw and install reading lamps near comfortable chairs. A fire screen is a must for safety; choose one that also contributes to the overall style of the room.

A quiet, elegant backdrop of taupe walls and creamy white woodwork stands back and listens as furniture and accessories carry on a lively conversation.

A round gilt mirror finds a perfect frame on the mantel wall. Even when the firebox is unlit, the glass-top table, hurricane jar, silver bucket, and wineglasses bring glint and shine to the space.

Rolled-arm seating signals comfort and a less formal feel than upholstered pieces with straight, tuxedo-style frames.

Brugge Bruges Bruges Brügge
Bruxelles Brussel Brussels Brüssel
Belgié Belgique Belgium Belgien

French style is enjoying a renaissance in popularity; one reason may be its flexibility. Can't fly to France to shop the local flea markets and stores? No problem. The style has recognizable forms and traits that can be found in American pieces with a kindred spirit.

creme fresh

1 — BACKGROUND

WALL AND TRIM COLORS cappuccino; cream-white

FLOOR COVERINGS hardwood flooring; antique area rug

2 — FURNITURE

SEATING upholstered pieces with curved wooden frames

TABLES wood side tables; metal and glass coffee table

3 — accessories

WELCOMING TOUCHES glass, pottery, and silver containers

NATURAL TOUCH fresh eucalyptus branches

EYE CANDY gilt mirror; fancy fabrics

A contemporary painting spices the room with color and counters the curved lines of the furniture with startling simplicity. Kilim toss pillows and a paisley throw repeat the rug colors.

At first glance this side table seems to have nothing to compare with the broken-out paneling. A second look reveals the same grain of the table, as curvy as the scrollwork on the chair arms.

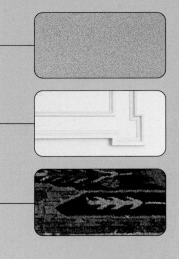

Look for architecture when you shop for a new home—it will give you a head start on a decorating scheme. The straitlaced English millwork that came with this house is an ideal backdrop for a collection of curvy French furniture. Sharing focal point status with the fireplace, the rug guides guests into the room and grounds the seating arrangement.

Arrange furniture in a U-shape around the fireplace. Pale linen upholsteries and a glass-top coffee table ensure that the Hariz rug gets the attention it deserves. The coffee table is a custom copy of a pricier piece; the end table is a catalog find.

Accessorize the room in keeping with the decorative style established by the softly curved furniture. Then add a surprise accessory or two to counter the theme—or merely to tease the eye or cause a turn in the conversation. In this room, the gilt mirror hints of France and quietly adds another curve to the space. Pillow fabrics and rounded vases also repeat the gracious European theme. However, on the wall to the right of the fireplace, a modern painting and a handcrafted side table, *opposite,* provoke discussion about modern art styles.

FURNITURE Search out authentic antique pieces at antiques stores or secondhand shops. Also check ebay.com, attend estate sales, or make bids at auctions. For look-alikes with similar lines, buy reproduction pieces from home stores or through catalogs. For artisan pieces, such as this handhewn side table, *left,* attend art markets, street fairs, and crafts galleries.

ACCESSORIES Let your instincts be your guide when choosing accent pieces. Keep in mind the basic recipe: a neutral backdrop, curvy furnishings, and a starring-role rug. Choose vases, vessels, and other art to complement the colors and shapes in the room.

Modern minimalism marries old-fashioned character in a Victorian flat. It's a new life for an old soul and a living room recipe that's easy to assemble.

second wind

1   BACKGROUND

WALL AND TRIM COLORS cream white; pale beige

WINDOW COVERINGS white venetian blinds

FLOOR COVERING dark wood planking

FIXED LIGHTING modern ceiling fixture

2   Furniture

SEATING modern chairs; floor cushions

TABLE modern coffee table

STORAGE antique pharmacy cabinet; wall shelving

3   accessories

PERSONAL COMFORTS animal-print chair cushions; fur floor-cushion covers

EYE CANDY glass bottles; framed prints; ceramics

WELCOMING TOUCH flowers in a glass vase

Paint a high ceiling a pale beige that calls attention to its distant beauty; paint the walls and woodwork a creamy white that makes the room grow wider visually. Hang three open shelves on a wall to expand storage and display space for collectibles; shelving also adds architecture to the room. Replace old-fashioned lighting with a modern chandelier. Clean and wax the dark wood flooring.

Place the coffee table directly under the ceiling fixture and it becomes the centerpiece for the room. Surround the dark wood coffee table with seating upholstered in light colors that almost disappear into the walls. This scheme of creamy white against dark wood forms the backdrop, and the furniture showcases a collection of accessories that have similar light/dark features. Roll in an antique pharmacy cabinet on wheels for additional collectible display and storage.

Add accessories that show your personal interests. Here, a collection of clear glass containers reflect sunlight from the bay window. White stoneware and porcelain bowls mix with the glassware and framed prints in a relaxed arrangement. To create your own arrangement, pick a theme or common denominator for the collection. For example, choose a textural theme, layering objects made of wood, wicker, and metal, or iron, glass, and paper. Establish a focal point with a prized object worthy of a starring role; then build around it, adding depth. Instead of a flat lineup, stagger glassware and framed photos in a front-to-back zigzag pattern. Leave breathing room between the items so shapely pieces can show off their curves.

Modern and Victorian styles work well together. The secret? Keep the background pattern to a minimum.

Open shelving in a stack of three adds architectural interest, storage for collectibles, and display space for precious finds.

Food for thought...

Well-balanced lighting layers three types of light: general (ambient) light, task light, and accent light. The right mix of lighting can bring "sunshine" to any room, create drama, visually alter room dimensions, and highlight your favorite things. An even distribution of general light is key. Task lighting illuminates reading, cooking, and work areas. Accent lighting draws attention to the most interesting and artful aspects of a room.

A low coffee table and dark wood floor draw the eye downward from the high ceiling, making the room feel more cozy and modern.

Faux paneling gives plain blue walls a lot more character.

Unframed art tacked loosely on the wall adds a casual note to the decor.

Use a cloth instead of a brush to give a softer look to a stencil. Dampen the cloth and wring it dry before painting. Rinse if it becomes too saturated with paint.

Curvy white furniture carries the soft, courtly look of Gustavian style.

A Swedish-inspired garland of painted leaves is a light alternative to an area rug.

Blue faux-paneled walls and a painted floor whip up a light and airy Swedish-style look.

over the border

 B a c k g r o u n d

WALL AND TRIM COLORS pale periwinkle blue; white

FLOOR COVERINGS white floor planking; painted floor design

FIXED LIGHTING window light

 F u r n i t u r e

SEATING slipcovered rolled-arm sofa; curvy wicker side chairs

TABLES pedestal table; round and rectangular side tables

 a c c e s s o r i e s

TASK LIGHTING table lamp

PERSONAL COMFORTS upholstered footstool; blue and white print pillows

EYE CANDY flowers; landscape prints on watercolor paper

Paint floor boards and trim with white deck paint. To create the pretend paneling, use a level and a No. 3 hard lead pencil or water-erasable sewing marker to mark the position of the chair rail (a standard height is 35 inches from the floor); also mark the positions of the panels below the chair rail. On the floor, draw a large oval or circle around the area you wish to define. From blank stencil plastic, cut a 24-inch-long chair rail stencil (to use repeatedly), a rectangular panel stencil, and leaf stencils of various sizes for the floor design. To paint, dip a lint-free cloth into acrylic paint (available at art and crafts supply stores); then blot it onto paper to remove most of the paint. Gently press the cloth to the wall or floor through the stencil opening. Remove the stencil and move it to the next position. When the floor design is complete, cover the entire floor with one or more coats of clear polyurethane.

Arrange seating pieces around the painted rug to create a spacious, reserved atmosphere. Place a 36-inch-diameter pedestal table in the center of the painted rug. Add a mix of round and rectangular side tables at convenient locations near seating pieces.

Choose blue and white patterns to cover comfortable throw pillows and footstools. For an inspiring coffee table display, buy decorating books that feature Scandinavian style. Tack watercolor prints on the wall with pushpins and set the tables with a lamp or two. Add large blue and white serving trays.

Timeless colors, traditional fabrics, and large-scale furnishings result in an eclectic, classically styled room that looks and feels bigger than it is.

small is savvy

 1 B A C K G R O U N D

WALL AND TRIM COLOR yellow-gold

FLOOR COVERING sisal carpeting

GENERAL LIGHTING classic floor lamp

 2 F u r n i t u r e

SEATING extra-deep sofa; natural wicker side chair

TABLES slipcovered ottoman; classical side table

STORAGE metal side table

 3 a c c e s s o r i e s

MOOD LIGHTING pillar candles on tall candlesticks;

can lights

PERSONAL COMFORTS pillows; throw

EYE CANDY urns; prints; statuary; columns; flowers

Paint walls yellow-gold—tiny rooms live large when coated in color that excites and ignites. With a satin-finish paint, cover base and crown moldings in the same color as the walls; the color continuity will make the room seem bigger. From a flooring gallery, order wall-to-wall sisal carpeting and have it professionally installed. Or purchase a room-size area rug to lay over an existing floor.

Furnish the space with an extra-deep sofa, a beefy ottoman, and a sturdy wicker armchair, keeping balanced proportions and comfort in mind. When you buy big, you need fewer pieces. Choose furniture with plain covers in warm, earthy browns; patterns visually arrest the eye and take up space. Arrange the seating pieces in an L-shape near a window to make a corner of comfort. Tuck in a table or two between the sofa and chair—a taller piece for holding decorative items and a shorter, modern table near the armchair for stacking a small library of books.

Classical accessories bring this room to life. First, arrange the lighting: Place a floor lamp at the end of the sofa farthest from the chair. Direct can lights upward along the sofa wall to create drama. Top the ottoman with a supersize tray and a pair of dramatic candlesticks. Hang a giant map over the sofa and add a medallion mirror. Next, add black-painted columns and garden statues to give the room classical architecture and a hint of Greek mythology. Finally, soften seating with some subtly patterned pillows and decorate tabletops with small items of interest, such as books, pictures, and plants. For special occasions, arrange flowers in an urn.

Like the rays of the sun, gold walls warm a space. The rich color reflects pools of light that radiate from lamps and candles.

A giant wall map broadens and heightens a small space.

Tall columns elevate an ordinary space.

Fewer, bigger furnishings eliminate clutter and give a room comfort and weight.

Food for thought...

To add an apartment above your garage, check with local officials first. Zoning regulations may pose a stumbling block, but many localities will grant a variance if you observe certain niceties, such as preserving a garage look and providing adequate off-street parking. Also inquire about fire codes for living quarters situated over a garage. Most require two exits and a fire wall between the garage and living space.

An empty corner makes room for a photo-frame floor screen.

Like bookends, pairs of lamps and armchairs bring balance and order to the arrangement.

A sleigh bed serves as a comfy sofa during the day. Drawers in the coffee table/chest store bed linens.

A studio apartment, built over the garage, is handy for long-term visitors—grandchildren, grown children, or an elderly parent.

LIVING OUT BACK

1 BACKGROUND

WALL AND TRIM COLOR white

WINDOW COVERINGS venetian blinds

FLOOR COVERINGS painted wood; woven area rug

FIXED LIGHTING overhead ceiling fixture

2 FURNITURE

SEATING sleigh bed; upholstered armchairs; dining chairs

TABLES end tables; glass-top dining table

STORAGE low chest of drawers (coffee table)

3 accessories

MOOD LIGHTING floor lamps; votive candles

PERSONAL COMFORTS throw pillows for sleigh bed

EYE CANDY corner photo screen; flowers in glass vase; porcelain serving pieces

Paint a blank canvas of white walls, ceilings, and floors inside the living space. Install a decorative overhead lighting fixture and hang outside-mount white wood or metal venetian blinds with white valances at the windows. Lay the large woven area rug on the floor to establish the seating area.

Place the low chest/coffee table in the center of the room on the area rug directly under the ceiling fixture. Face the drawers toward the door so that the sleigh bed and the wall behind it become the focal point for the room. Center the sleigh bed/sofa along the back side of the coffee table, leaving an 18 to 24-inch walkway between the pieces. Position two upholstered armchairs opposite each other diagonally across the room. Place the dining table and chairs in the leftover space near the door and settle small, round end tables near the armchairs.

Arrange accessories. Fill the empty corner at the back wall with a photograph-filled floor screen; the screen also creates a nook for the armchair nearby. Place a pair of matching lamps at opposite ends of the sleigh bed and fluff up the bed with cushiony comforts. When guests move in for a weekend, week, or month, cut flowers from the garden and arrange them in clear glass containers. In the coffee table drawers, store the linens, votive candles for special occasions, and all the conveniences your apartment guests will need.

DINING rooms

No matter who comes to your table or what's on the menu, you deserve a dining area that reflects your decorating taste and lifestyle. To stir up a new dining style of your own, study this chapter for inspiration. The first part of the chapter reveals how the three basic ingredients—background, furniture, and accessories—blend together to make this sunny indoor pavilion dining room. The rest of the chapter serves up additional recipes for a variety of tasty dining rooms. Which room appeals most to your decorating appetite?

This recipe for dining calls for combining modern with traditional—and adding a dash of sheer romance. Season it with an edgy antique and you'll end up with a deliciously original American room.

saffron sunshine

 1 BACKGROUND

WALL COLORS dark, medium, and light yellows

WINDOW COVERINGS AND ROOM DIVIDER sheer white panels

FLOOR COVERINGS floor paint; woven runner

FIXED LIGHTING hallway wall fixtures

 2 FURNITURE

TABLE 32x80-inch solid-core door with handmade base

CHAIRS woven wicker and metal

STORAGE metal baker's rack; miniature wall-hung drawers

 3 accessories

MOOD LIGHTING ceiling-hung candleholders

TABLEWARE serving pieces in glass, ceramic, and metal

PERSONAL TOUCHES antique gas-station numbers; fresh flowers from the garden

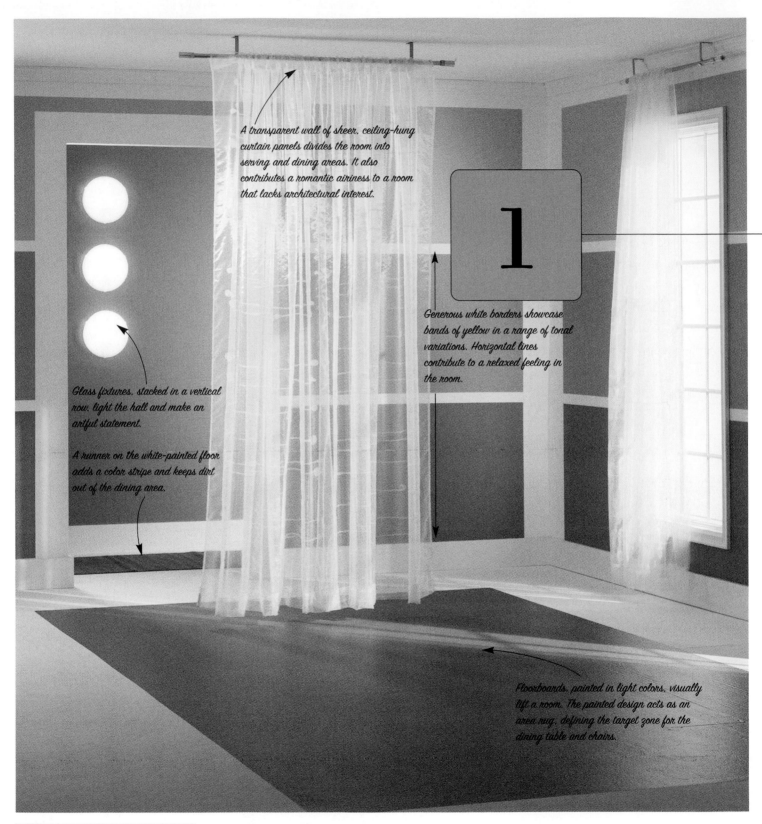

A transparent wall of sheer, ceiling-hung curtain panels divides the room into serving and dining areas. It also contributes a romantic airiness to a room that lacks architectural interest.

1

Generous white borders showcase bands of yellow in a range of tonal variations. Horizontal lines contribute to a relaxed feeling in the room.

Glass fixtures, stacked in a vertical row, light the hall and make an artful statement.

A runner on the white-painted floor adds a color stripe and keeps dirt out of the dining area.

Floorboards, painted in light colors, visually lift a room. The painted design acts as an area rug, defining the target zone for the dining table and chairs.

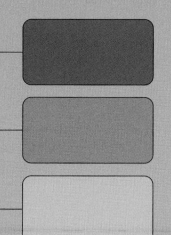

WALLS To select colors for banded walls, examine the paint strips at paint stores. Choose the strip that appeals to you most; buy a range of three colors positioned next to each other on the strip. This system of color selection works for any color, with any paint strip.

B a c k g r o u n d Like white flour for baking, white paint is a decorating staple, especially when you have white walls or moldings that need freshening from time to time. Choose one white only (there are dozens) and stick to it, using it throughout your house and keeping it on hand for touch-ups. You'll need satin or high-gloss paint for trim and a flat or eggshell finish for walls.

To paint color bands on a white wall, you'll need 2-inch-wide painter's tape, and a level, ruler, and pencil. Using these tools, mark the walls and establish 6-inch-wide borders at each corner, around doorways, at the ceiling edge, and along the baseboards. Next, divide the remaining wall height into three equal parts, allowing for 2-inch-wide bands of white between the colors. With painter's tape, mask off the white sections. Paint the remaining areas with your color choices and remove the tape.

For the floor, use the same procedure as for the wall, except mask off 18- or 24-inch-wide white borders around the painted faux rug.

To hang the curtains and room divider, screw the curtain rod brackets to the ceiling instead of over the window frames. Use anchored screws for security.

WINDOWS, DIVIDER You'll need long panels of sheer fabric that hang almost to the floor. For example, if your ceiling is 8-feet high, you'll need panels that are 7½-feet long. This allows 3 inches of space at the ceiling for the rod brackets and 3 inches of clearance at the floor. Measure the height of your walls to determine the panel length. Substitute hand-sewn panels for ready-mades, if desired.

FLOOR COVERINGS Purchase a runner in a color close to the paint colors. To create a faux rug with paint, choose a tone slightly darker than the three wall colors. Ask the paint store to mix the color in a washable floor or deck paint that will hold up under heavy use. Avoid varnishes or finishes with yellowing qualities.

A baker's rack behind the curtain divider provides a semi-private service bar for mixing drinks or stashing supplies. Glass shelves keep the piece looking light.

FURNITURE Unless you're picnicking, you need a table, chairs, and storage to share and enjoy food in comfort. When you add these basic building blocks to your dining space, you immediately gain a sense of order, style, and luxury. Even when the furnishings are utilitarian, organizing a dining space adds further gratification to one of life's most delightful pleasures—eating.

To make the handcrafted table, *opposite*, you'll need a 32×80-inch, solid-core door; 20 feet of 2×2-inch pine stock; 8 long screws; and gray deck paint for a sturdy, washable surface finish. Cut the 2-inch pine into four 28-inch legs, two 25-inch end rails, and two 38-inch side rails. Assemble the table base by screwing the two end rails to the legs 6 inches below the tops of the legs. Screw the side rails between the two sets of legs to complete the table base. Paint all table parts. When the paint is dry, lay the door on top of the base, centering it on the legs so that it overhangs 1½ inches on each side.

Substitution: 1 door + 4 legs = table

Instead of building the table base shown here, purchase four legs with tabletop attachments to fasten to a solid-core door (you'll find them at home improvement centers). Or check out the variety of legs offered at **tablelegsonline.com**. When choosing a door that will become a tabletop, opt for a narrow one—32 inches wide—to avoid the clumsy, 1970s "table-made-from-a-door" look.

2

Small chests of drawers hung side by side on the wall make a mini-sideboard and add silver-leaf sparkle to the room.

Build, buy, or inherit a table to seat at least six. The best buy is a table with leaves, which allows for expansion.

Light, wicker chairs suggest informality; upholstered chairs provide a formal feel. To protect a floor from scratches, put felt disks or sliders on the bottom ends of chair legs.

Masquerading as a napkin ring, this curtain ring and clip also make a clever place card holder.

Julie

One small chandelier by itself has little visual impact. Several massed together create a more dramatic effect.

3

Votive candleholders on a miniature sideboard add glitter and sparkle.

Fill a drawer with fabric napkins in dining room colors. Dark napkins create formality; bright ones lighten the mood of a meal.

accessories Personality comes to light in a room with small functional, decorative items that please the senses and express your point of view.

To make computer-generated place cards, print the names of guests on white paper (the ideal place card is the same size as a business card). Cut out the cards and take them to a print shop for lamination, or finish them yourself with a laminating kit. Trim the laminated cards on a paper cutter, leaving a $\frac{1}{4}$-inch margin around the paper edges. Fasten the cards to clip-curtain rings and slip the rings over rolled-up dinner napkins.

To create a candelight chandelier, combine a small beaded candle chandelier with two glass flower vases made to hang on wall hooks. Attach a delicate chain (available at hardware stores) to each vase and the chandelier and loop the chains over plant hooks securely fastened to the ceiling above the dining room table. Fill the vases with water and add floating candles.

To frost a mini-sideboard with silver leaf, buy gold-leaf adhesive, a booklet of $5\frac{1}{2}$-inch-square silver leaf (one booklet contains 25 squares), and a soft, long bristled brush. You'll find all of these in crafts supply stores. First, remove the drawers and paint the outer surfaces and edges of the empty chests black. Allow the paint to dry for 48 hours. Follow the manufacturer's instructions on the package of silver leaf for applying it to the drawer fronts, and the sides and top of each chest unit. Tip: Using waxed paper between your fingertips and the silver-leaf keeps the delicate material from clinging to your hands instead of to the unit.

Food for thought...

The dining room, so often used for entertaining, calls out for dramatic lighting. Instead of hanging one fixture in the middle of the ceiling, use a variety of fixtures to serve your practical and decorative needs. For example, balance light from a hanging fixture with recessed ceiling lights that illuminate artwork, brighten a buffet, or accentuate the appealing dimensions of the space. A broad expanse of mirrors doubles the illumination and the apparent size of the room.

Give a mostly modern room an edge with antique metal numbers. Adding the right seasoning puts zest into any room.

If your floor plan includes a formal dining room, keep the mood light with outdoorsy chairs and a round table.

DINING LIGHT

 1 B a c k g r o u n d

TRIM COLOR bright white

WALL COLOR soft toffee, caramel, or taupe

WINDOW COVERINGS sheer lace panels on white rods

FLOOR COVERINGS wood flooring; Asian-style area rug

 2 F u r n i t u r e

TABLE round glass-top table with curved base

CHAIRS woven wicker with curved lines

STORAGE built-in buffet

 3 a c c e s s o r i e s

MOOD LIGHTING wall sconce; natural light

TABLEWARE floral china; rose-color glassware

FINER TOUCHES lace napkins; mirror; flowers; glass vase

VINTAGE PIECES silver tray; antique clock

Choose a bright white paint for all the woodwork in the room, including fixed furniture such as the buffet and curtain rods. Once painted, window frames, rods, door frames, and built-in furniture pieces become the clean, white "bones" of the room—the skeleton that supports the rest of the furnishings. Flesh out the bones with a quiet neutral wall paint that contrasts with the woodwork without overpowering it. Add delicate lace curtains to soften the window frames. Lay a traditional area rug on the floor to define the dining area and bring a bit of color and texture to the mostly white room.

Arrange a round table and wicker chairs in the center of the dining room. A round table allows for additional seating as necessary. Placing it in the middle of the room opens up plenty of space for pulling chairs away from the table. Chances are, a general lighting fixture is already in place in the center of the ceiling; placing the table directly beneath it is a tried-and-true furniture-arranging solution.

Choose pretty floral porcelain plates, cups, and vases for table use. Add rose-color stemware, white napkins, and silver accessories to keep the room looking light and airy. One or two well-chosen dark pieces, such as an antique clock, provide a little contrast to the color play. Install a bevel-edged mirror at the back of the buffet, using white framing or mirror clips available at home centers.

Extra-long cotton lace panels, hung from rods that graze the ceiling, allow sunlight to filter into the room.

Midtone walls surrounding bright white woodwork add to the crisp, fresh, and airy look of the room.

Wall sconces, like candles, bring romance to evening meals.

A mirror behind a buffet shelf suggests a pass-through to the adjacent room, visually opening up the space.

The gentle weave of wicker brings a friendly texture to the space, providing contrast to the smooth walls and slick glass tabletop.

Hang lace panels from white curtain clips and a wooden rod. Or hang lace tablecloths for a similar effect at your windows.

Three pendent lights hung over a long, formal table make it seem more relaxed. Using two or four lamps (even numbers) would add more formality.

A smooth laminate floor underscores the slickness of this mostly modern room.

For minimalist table settings, combine square plates with round bowls. Fold in a dash of energy with persimmon-color napkins.

The bold pairing of a vintage table and modern chairs has worked in dining rooms for decades. Here's how.

modern mix

1 **BACKGROUND**

WALL AND TRIM COLOR warm white

FLOOR COVERING wood planking or wood laminate

FIXED LIGHTING striped pendants

2 **FURNITURE**

TABLE 1940s Heywood-Wakefield extendable table

CHAIRS Jesus Gasca's modern chairs

STORAGE wheeled cart; wall-hung shelves

3 **accessories**

ART framed poster or enlarged photo illustration; light-color objects for shelving display

TABLEWARE dark and light pieces; clear glass stemware

NATURAL TOUCHES fresh-cut greenery

Use one color for walls and trim so window frames and walls unite. Choose a hue that recedes—a light color or white—and walls will stay quietly in the background. Light walls will provide contrast to dark or midtone furnishings. (Think of the furnishings as sculpture in a white-walled gallery.) Leave windows uncovered for minimum distraction and maximum sunlight; ground the room with a dark wood laminate floor. Hang three pendent lights from the ceiling and install dimmers so that you can shift the dining room mood from open to intimate.

Arrange a 1940s table and new, curvy chairs along the length of the room, centering the dining area under the pendants. Keep the leaves of the table in place so you can enjoy the elegance of your vintage piece to the fullest. Acquire a rolling wooden cart for tableside service and easy transport of food and dirty dishes between the dining room and kitchen. Mount a three-tiered, light-color set of shelves on the wall to hold light-color objects. Design tip: Dark objects on pale shelves and walls shout for attention; white objects blend and unite with a white wall, creating a richer, more sophisticated display.

Choose white dinner plates and dark, contrasting place mats for the table. On a rectangular table, layer square and rectangular dishes and mats on the tabletop for a delightfully modern invitation to dinner. Add wall art that can serve as a focal point.

Three door headers, converted to plate rails, turn a divider wall into a cupboard and set the tone for a loft dining space that nourishes diners with minimalist leanings.

BOLD PLATED

 1 **BACKGROUND**

WALL COLOR your choice of paint

FIXED ARCHITECTURE industrial vents; divider wall

ADDED ARCHITECTURE door header cupboard

FIXED LIGHTING window light; overhead fixtures

 2 **FURNITURE**

TABLE antique gateleg table

CHAIRS brushed metal

STORAGE door header cupboard

 3 **accessories**

TABLEWARE white china; clear glasses; antique fruit bowl

FABRICS matelassé tablecloth; dot-and-stripe napkins

NATURAL TOUCHES cut flowers; fruit

Make a focal point with paint, lumber, and a divider wall. First, paint the wall in a color that suits the mood you want in your dining area. To make the plate rails/"cupboard," look for old headers at architectural salvage stores. Or make your own from hardware store materials. These 36-inch-long rails have backs made from 1×6 clear pine boards topped by 1×3 boards, which have been routed for plates. Center the top rails on the backs, with back edges flush. Fasten with wood screws and trim with decorative molding (use a miter saw to cut the molding; then glue and nail it in place). Paint the plate rails with primer and two coats of white enamel. Countersink two sets of screw holes on the face of the backboards, positioning the holes $1\frac{1}{2}$ inches in from each end. Screw the plate rails to the wall, leaving 12 inches between each rail. Wood buttons (available in the dowel section of home centers) make snappy covers for screw holes.

Arrange a table and chairs to squarely face the plate display rather than setting them at an angle. Select metal chairs that contrast with the antique (take a decorating cue from the metal vents overhead) to keep your choice in line with the overall look of the space.

Choose white dinner plates for table use and for wall decor. Set on the door headers, the plates become a focal point in the room. On the table, they function as frames for beautifully prepared food. A white tablecloth expands the pure and simple look. For variety in color and texture, add patterned napkins and garden flowers in clear glass vases.

A divider wall creates intimacy in an open space, such as a loft. Old-fashioned door headers, used in a new way, create architecture and fixed storage.

Get in the groove: Use a router to cut a trough in the top of each plate rail. The trough keeps plates from slipping.

White plates gain visual interest in repetition. They also function at the table.

Simple-chic style combines inexpensive, basic materials with sophisticated design. Look for affordable copycat versions of designer chairs.

A large mirror reflects an elegant dining scene and heightens the glamour of the room.

A chandelier dimmer switch (a $2 investment) creates flattering and intimate mood lighting.

Food for thought...

Consider these two tips for decorating on a shoestring:
1. Pour your money into paint; it's an inexpensive way to create dramatic change in a room. 2. Shop garage sales, antiques stores, and flea markets for bargains. If you're thinking about buying something, buy it! It's likely to work somewhere in your home, but not likely to be available if you decide to buy it later. Accept dings or minor damage to furniture. You'll save money and you'll enjoy a slightly worn piece more because you're not afraid to use it.

Red walls energize conversation, boost the spirits, and romance a meal. Red is also known for its power to stir the appetite.

A couple of cans of paint—in a shade called "roasted pepper"— create flaming red walls and give a dining room an appetizing boost of color.

cafe provence

1 BACKGROUND

WALL COLOR warm red

FLOOR COVERINGS wood flooring; tapestry area rug

FIXED LIGHTING chandelier

2 Furniture

TABLE antique table with crackle finish

CHAIRS curvy chairs with classic French lines

STORAGE antique sideboard with painted finish

3 accessories

MOOD LIGHTING pillar candles on large stands

TABLEWARE floral china; tapestry runner

FRENCH CAFE TOUCHES rooster figure; painted tray

NATURAL TOUCH fresh-cut flowers in a garden urn

Paint a focal point wall in a warm red color. Acquire a prize chandelier to replace an ordinary lighting fixture and haunt consignment stores until you find a beautiful tapestry rug for the dining room floor.

Add a crackle finish to an ordinary table. Apply a specially formulated crackle medium (available at crafts supply stores) over a base coat of paint; then apply a top coat in a contrasting color over the cured medium. The crackle medium causes the top coat paint to stretch and split so that some of the base coat becomes visible. For the look shown here, paint the table base with a dark brown, apply the crackling medium (following label instructions), and finish with a top coat of cream-color paint. For a classic French touch, re-cover dining chair seats with black and cream checkered fabric: Unscrew the seats from the chair frames and stretch pieces of fabric around the seats. Use a stapler to fasten the fabric edges to the undersides of the chairs. For storage of table linens, move in a painted sideboard.

Bring on Provençal style. That means a rooster figure, giant pillars on candlestands, and fresh flowers in an ancient-looking urn (which is actually a brand-new piece). Hang a giant mirror that will reflect the faces of your friends around the table.

Both playful and pedigreed, this dining room holds classic furnishings that are dressed down in crisp, easy-to-live-with neutrals.

TABLE DE CHARME

1 BACKGROUND

WALL AND TRIM COLOR white

WINDOW COVERINGS white plantation shutters

FLOOR COVERING high-gloss painted planks

FIXED LIGHTING steel candle chandelier with swirl design

2 Furniture

TABLE neoclassic table base; glass tabletop

CHAIRS slipper chairs with white pleated slipcovers

STORAGE distressed corner cabinet

3 accessories

MOOD LIGHTING candles; inset lighting in corner cabinet

TABLEWARE blue and white china; etched glassware

VINTAGE TOUCHES porcelain platters; crystal; paintings

FINER TOUCHES cut flowers; white linens; glass beads

Whitewash the background—walls, ceiling, crown and base moldings, window frames, doors, and floor—with clean, bright paint. For the walls and ceiling, use a flat or eggshell finish. Apply the same white in a semigloss finish on all the trim. For the floor, apply several coats of a hardworking floor or deck paint in a high-gloss, easy-to-clean finish. When choosing the paint, ask your paint dealer for advice on which paint to use for the various parts of the room. Fasten the chandelier to the ceiling over the center of the table area. Note: The best place for a table is a bit to the side or at one end of the room, away from the door(s), to allow for easy traffic past the table. Also, allow space around the table for comfortable seating and movement of chairs (at least 24 inches behind each chair). Install inside-mount plantation shutters in windows.

Move furniture into the pure white envelope of space you've painted. Center the table under the chandelier and place the cabinet in a nearby corner. Dress the slipper chairs in loose white-linen slipcovers with slightly formal pleated backs.

Install lighting inside the cabinet—at both the top and under the shelves. The small lights show off displayed china and add sparkle to the room. Mixing oval and round pieces with rectangular artwork creates a lively arrangement for hanging on the wall. Loop glass-bead garlands through the arms of the chandelier and attach clear glass teardrop ornaments. Set the table with white cotton lace linens, blue and white china, and candles in crystal holders.

Round and oval platters and a curvy chandelier balance the straight lines of architecture, picture frames, and boxy furniture pieces.

A tall corner cabinet anchors the room and gives it a dignified and glamorous focal point.

Pleated slipcovers have a crisp yet casual style.

A glossy white painted floor visually lifts a room.

Substitution: slipcovers

The bleachable white cotton slipcovers shown here make maintenance easy. If you want a warmer look, switch out the slipcovers for a cozier set, perhaps a blue and white toile. Have them custom-made, sew them yourself from a fabric-store pattern, or check mail-order catalogs that offer basic slipper chairs and a wardrobe of slipcovers to fit them.

Replace the wooden louvers with sheer fabric panels. Sew 2-inch-wide rod pockets at the ends of each fabric panel so the panels pull taut when shirred onto the dowels and slipped under the curves of the opened screw eyes.

Sheer curtain panels, repeated in accordion-style "window walls", shelter an airy, inviting dining area while letting in the light.

Plants with large rounded leaves and relaxed natural shapes balance the angular lines of manufactured furnishings. Plants, generally thought of as accessories, also play a rhythmical background role.

Mixing materials, such as wood, wicker, and glass, creates textural variety that pleases the eye and the hands.

An extended window treatment is the main ingredient in this recipe for dining. Bifold doors embrace a dining set in front of a bay window. Try this recipe for daylight dining.

Two For Tea

 1 BACKGROUND

WALL COLOR off-white

WINDOW COVERINGS sheer white panels; trifold "window walls"

FLOOR COVERINGS hardwood flooring; sisal area rug

 2 FURNITURE

TABLE square wood-and-glass table

CHAIRS woven wicker and wood

 3 accessories

MOOD LIGHTING natural light

TABLEWARE white bowls for between-meals centerpiece

NATURAL TOUCHES green plant; fresh fruit; green-glazed ceramic pots

Fill the sections of a bay window with panels of discount store sheers hung on tension rods. To extend the window treatment on each end, make two accordion-style walls. You'll need three sets of louvered bifolds, an extra hinge, three ¼-inch-diameter, 36-inch-long dowels, and 24 brass screw eyes. Separate one set of doors and use the hinges to join one door to each remaining bifold set, being careful to attach them so they fold in the appropriate direction (accordion style). Remove the top rails from each door and slide out the louver blades. Use wood filler in the grooves left by the blades; let filler dry and sand smooth. Replace the top rails and paint the doors. From the dowels, cut 12 fabric rods that measure ½ inch less than the width of the openings. Install brass screw eyes into the tops and bottoms of the louver openings, 1 inch away from each side. With pliers, open the screw eyes so the dowels can slip inside the brass loops. Shirr transparent fabric onto the dowels (see detail, *opposite*).

Use a matching pair of chairs to serve a tiny table for two. Tuck the dining set into the intimate alcove created by the extended window treatment. Aim for contrast when pairing your table and chairs. Here wicker chairs introduce a rustic texture to contrast with the smooth wood and glass of the table.

Add natural accessories in monochromatic tones, such as green plants and planters along with a white bowl filled with green apples. These simple, ordinary, affordable elements contribute to the tranquil setting.

Weave together indoors and outdoors with floral fabrics, brightly colored dishes, potted plants, and paintings that echo the sunny garden beyond.

garden party

1 BACKGROUND

WALL AND TRIM COLOR creamy white

WINDOW COVERINGS vintage floral pleated panels

FLOOR COVERINGS wood planking or wood laminate

FIXED LIGHTING chandelier

2 FURNITURE

TABLE round country table with distressed white finish

CHAIRS green woven wicker with fabric seats

STORAGE wood nightstand

3 accessories

TABLEWARE bright dishes; glassware; floral table covering

NATURAL TOUCHES floral pillows; flower paintings; floral lampshades

FINER TOUCHES antique flatware; steel curtain rods

Paint a soft backdrop with creamy white paints—a semigloss finish for moldings and window frames, an eggshell or flat finish for the walls. Hang new or vintage floral curtain panels on stainless-steel rods from clip rings. If you have carpet in the dining room, consider replacing it with do-it-yourself wood laminate flooring from a home center or have the replacement done by professionals. Unlike carpet, which requires steam-cleaning, a wood floor is easily maintained.

Center the round table under the chandelier and position new or vintage wicker porch chairs around it. To provide storage in a small dining room such as this one, place a nightstand close to the table.

Toss a vintage curtain panel onto the table for a quirky yet coordinated look. Wrap seat cushions with floral fabrics (if you mix patterns, keep the colors in the same palette) and add pillow backrests. Stash linens in the nightstand and pot some plants for the dining area—they'll bring the outdoors in. Shop flea markets for funky tableware in bright solid colors. To make the chandelier lampshades, purchase plain shades that come with a self-adhesive kit for custom covering. Using the pattern provided in the kit, cut lampshade covers from floral fabric and mount them on the shades (following the instructions that come with the kit).

New shades and crystals are a fresh lift for an old chandelier.

A large-scale flower painting repeats the garden theme.

Metal awnings shelter an indoor setting and provide an unexpected advantage: When raindrops fall on the metal roof, the boundary between in and out disappear.

Convert an old icebox into a kitchen display and storage area by removing its upper doors. Floral fabric shelf-liners and towels coordinate with dining room materials. Bright picnicware gives a punch of color.

Push a drop-leaf table against the wall as a serving console. When a crowd larger than eight gathers, pull out the drop-leaf for extra dining space.

A reproduction iron chandelier with crystal swags balances elegance and rusticity.

Black paint on trim and furniture pieces draws strong structural lines.

An antique bowl conveys an old-world mood and fits the scale of the room.

A banquet table offers the right amount of mass in a large-volume space. It balances the 16-foot-high ceiling, luring the eye back down to earth with strong autumnal hues.

In a high-ceilinged room or in a loft space without walls, large furnishings look better than smaller pieces. They fill the wide-open space and absorb any feeling of emptiness in the room.

Banquet Hall

 1 BACKGROUND

WALLS natural blond brick

WINDOW COVERINGS sheer white panels

FLOOR COVERINGS wood planking; large area rug

FIXED LIGHTING chandelier

 2 FURNITURE

TABLE large rectangular wood table

CHAIRS wood chairs with curved lines

STORAGE drop-leaf table; leaded-glass highboy cabinet

 3 accessories

MOOD LIGHTING taper candles in silver candleholders

TABLEWARE antique flatware; crystal; silver; china

EUROPEAN ACCENTS wooden trencher; silver tea service; clocks; vases; framed prints; tapestry runner

Underscore the architecture of the large space by painting the trim with black paint; this provides contrast to the natural blond brick walls. If you have nonbrick walls, paint them in a complementary Tuscany gold. Center the chandelier above the table space to make the area a focal point—a feat especially important in a space with no interior walls. Define the dining space with a large area rug; this is essential for distinguishing the dining area from other areas in a loft. Hang sheer panels from the tops of the windows and sweep them elegantly to the side with metal tiebacks to admit maximum natural light.

Center the banquet table and chairs on the rug under the chandelier and place the tall storage cabinet against the wall next to the window. To balance the height and mass of the highboy, position a drop-leaf table on the other side of the window and pair it with a mirror or framed piece of art.

Lay a tapestry runner along the length of the table, centering the fabric on the table surface. Top it with a large trencher as a centerpiece that you can leave empty or fill to the brim with natural objects. Tie cushions on the chair seats. Gather old crystal, china, and silver (check flea markets and secondhand shops for the best buys) and display them in the highboy. Top off the overall look with accent pieces, such as an interesting clock or a painted wooden tray.

KITCHENS

Besides your favorite cup of java, popular coffeehouses serve up comfortable seating, chalkboard menus, and a generous helping of hospitality. This kitchen is total takeout—its design lifted straight from coffeehouse decor. Learn how to create coffeehouse spirit in your kitchen.

COFFEEHOUSE BLEND

 BACKGROUND

WALL, TRIM, AND DOOR COLORS butter-cream; tan; rice-white; ice green; black chalkboard paint

WINDOW COVERINGS metallic miniblinds

FLOOR COVERING white oak laminate

 FURNITURE

FIXED standard base cabinets; wine-color countertop and coffee bar; aluminum suspension rails

FREESTANDING bar-height chairs; worktable with hanging pot rack; serving tray

 accessories

TASK LIGHTING stainless-steel pendent lamp

COOKWARE AND TABLEWARE stainless-steel pots, pans, trays; cookbook and plate rack; white china; glass cups

ACCENTS black and cream linens; clock; art; flowers

The kitchen—action zone and heart of the home—houses dozens of small items used to assemble and serve meals. In this chapter, you'll find room recipes that value the decorating potential of these utilitarian kitchen objects. You'll learn how to store such items in fashionable and functional ways. You'll also find ways to organize and keep clutter at bay despite all the cooking, meeting, eating, and communicating that goes on in this multitasking center of your home.

Garden Pizza

Lay out 2 packages Crescent Rolls on 15½ x 10½-inch cookie sheet. Bake according to package directions; cool.
—Cheese layer—
8 oz. cream cheese
½ c. salad dressing
1 t. onion flakes
½ t. each garlic, salt
Blend and spread on cooled crust.
—toppings—
1 c. chopped green pepper
1 c. chopped onion
1 c. chopped tomatoes
1 c. chopped black olives
Sprinkle on top and refrigerate
for several hours
before serving.

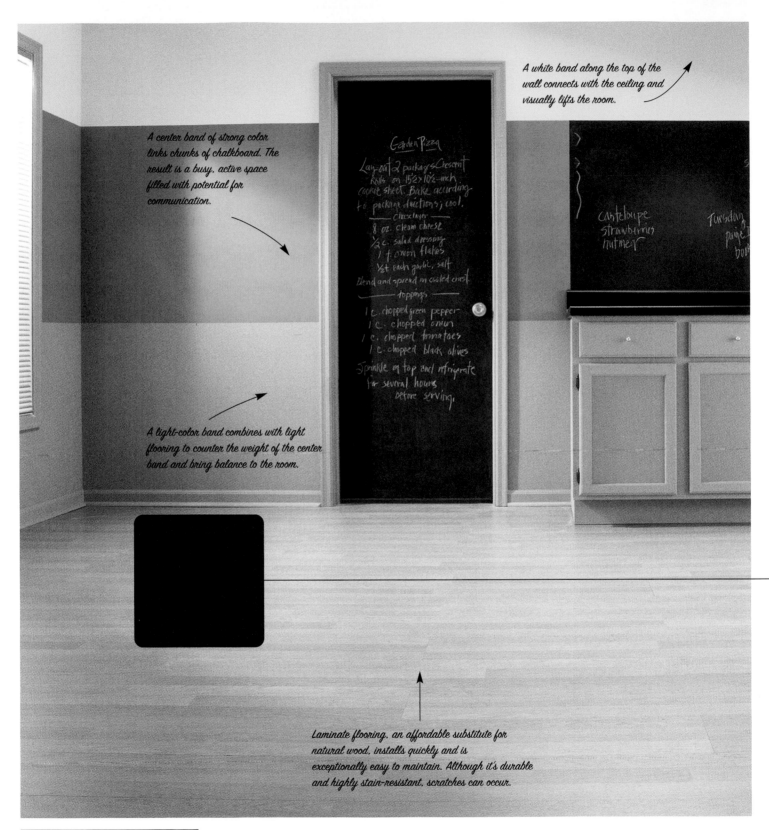

A white band along the top of the wall connects with the ceiling and visually lifts the room.

A center band of strong color links chunks of chalkboard. The result is a busy, active space filled with potential for communication.

A light-color band combines with light flooring to counter the weight of the center band and bring balance to the room.

Laminate flooring, an affordable substitute for natural wood, installs quickly and is exceptionally easy to maintain. Although it's durable and highly stain-resistant, scratches can occur.

BACKGROUND In most kitchens, fixed cabinetry comes with the space and can be considered part of the background ingredient of decorating. To alter the cabinets—with paint, new doors, or new countertops—include them in your background decorating plan. If you like the fixed cabinets as they are, integrate them into the color palette. This kitchen redo began with the removal of all upper cabinetry, the installation of new countertops, and a plan to paint the base cabinets the same color as the walls for a seamless, banded look.

To paint this background design, mark two horizontal lines around the room with pencil, one line 24 inches below the ceiling and the other about 35 inches from the floor (right below the fixed cabinetry countertops). Use a level to ensure straightness. Decide on chalkboard locations and mark their vertical boundaries. Mask off the top section with painter's tape and paint the top with a rice color paint in an eggshell finish; remove the tape. Mask off the bottom section and cover it with eggshell-finish butter-cream paint; remove the tape. Paint all moldings and cabinetry in semigloss butter-cream. When the paint is dry, mask off the inserts on the cabinet doors and paint them with tan semigloss paint. Remove the tape and allow the paint to dry for 24 hours. Mask off the middle wall section and fill in the ice green color band; remove the tape. Following the directions on the can of chalkboard paint, mask off and paint the chalkboard sections in the middle band. Remove the tape.

WALLS Examine the coordinating color cards that paint companies provide in stores. They are intended to make color selection easier and to suggest coordinating choices. For chalkboard paint, check crafts supply stores, where you will also find white chalk and chalkboard erasers. **Tip:** Prevent the ghost effect of the first words you write on a newly painted chalkboard by prepping it before you write on it. To prep, use the side of a chalk stick to completely cover the board with chalk; then wipe down the board with a soft rag.

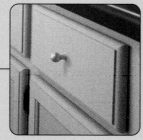

WINDOWS, CUPBOARDS Buy inside-mount miniblinds with aluminum or metallic blades to continue the utilitarian look. To keep the blinds shiny, clean them with the soft-fiber fingers of a blind duster. The duster works best when used frequently— before heavy dust builds up. To replace countertops, choose from color samples at a home center and order them custom-made and professionally installed. Replace outdated hardware with new knobs in brushed nickel or silver metal.

FLOOR COVERING Home improvement centers and flooring galleries offer many color choices in wood laminate flooring that you can install yourself. Alternatively, the home center or flooring gallery can install it for you.

A red countertop visually links the coffee bar with matching cabinet countertops, providing continuity in the overall kitchen design.

Furniture Restaurant-style furniture is fun—fun to find and fun to use. It adds a festive eating-out mood to an eat-in kitchen and inspires new ways to prepare and serve food. To find restaurant-style furniture, look in the Yellow Pages for a restaurant supply store near you. You'll find worktables, serving trays and stands, tables, and chairs. At the same time, you'll see ideas for the accessory part of this decorating plan: china, glassware, chef-size cooking pots and pans, and a great array of utensils. For bar-height stools and chairs, check any of your favorite furniture stores. Build a long shelf from wood and buy galvanized steel or aluminum mounting strips for storing and displaying wall accessories above the base cabinets.

To make the coffee bar, *right,* order a custom tabletop at the same time you order new countertops. This one measures 27×47 inches and has 38-inch-long wooden legs made from a 2×2 (attached to the underside of the tabletop with wood blocks and screws). The table is screwed to the wall through a rail attached to the underside at the table end. Also available is an adjustable bar-height leg in stainless steel that comes with an attachment for fastening it to the underside of the table. Check Internet sources for a bar-height leg in chrome or steel. Or order a complete ready-to-assemble counter unit from a catalog.

Substitutions: cushioned comfort

High barstools are only one option. Coffee houses sometimes offer comfy upholstered seating too: Velvety armchairs or built-in banquettes cozy up to tiny round bistro tables. If you have space at one end of your kitchen, move in two cushy armchairs and a side table. If you don't have much space, use a small bistro table-and-chairs set. Or consider buying an upholstered cafe booth from a restaurant supply store.

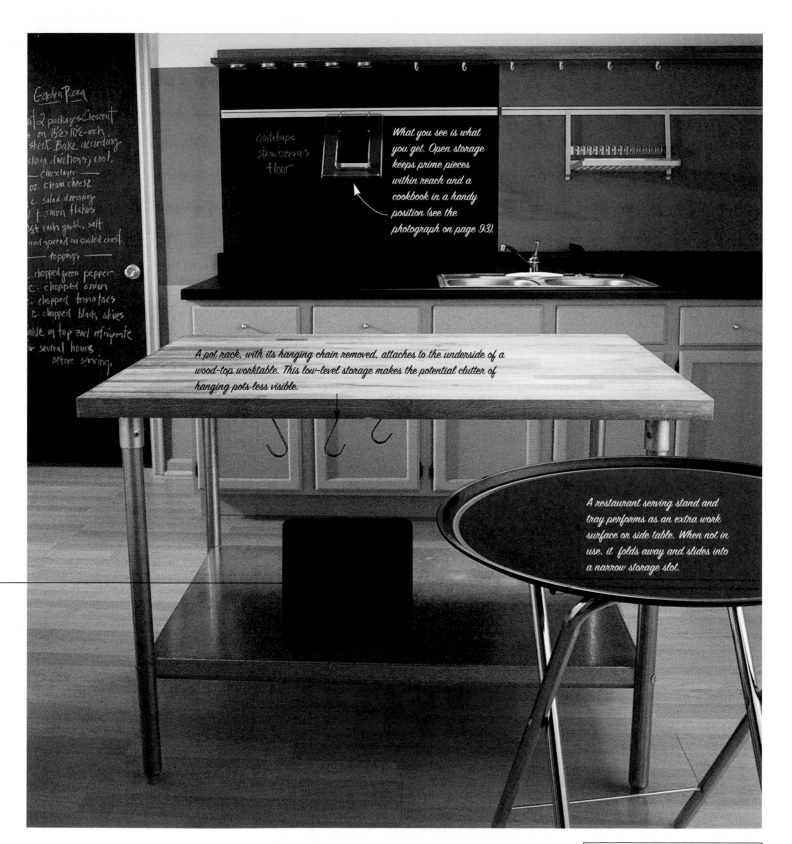

Garden Pizza

...of 2 packages Crescent
... on 15½x10½-inch
... sheet. Bake according
...ckage directions; cool.

— Cheese layer —

...oz. cream cheese
... c. salad dressing
... t. onion flakes
...ast each garlic, salt
...and spread on cooled crust.

— toppings —

... chopped green pepper
... c. chopped onion
... chopped tomatoes
... c. chopped black olives

...nkle on top and refrigerate
...r several hours
...before serving.

cantelope
strawberries
flour

What you see is what you get. Open storage keeps prime pieces within reach and a cookbook in a handy position (see the photograph on page 93).

A pot rack, with its hanging chain removed, attaches to the underside of a wood-top worktable. This low-level storage makes the potential clutter of hanging pots less visible.

A restaurant serving stand and tray performs as an extra work surface or side table. When not in use, it folds away and slides into a narrow storage slot.

Antique school slates serve as place mats.

Red-orange flowers pop an accent color into the room. Clear plastic water bottles, recycled as vases, sparkle on a countertop.

Recycled grocery-store sauce jars, with their screw lids attached to the underside of a shelf, store a variety of coffee beans. Safety hooks hold cups.

snickerdoodle

chocolate raspberry truffle

emerald cream

french roast

a c c e s s o r i e s In a kitchen like this, everyday utensils are all the decoration you need. Avoid countertop chaos and shelving clutter by planning a limited, cohesive palette of colors and materials: clear glass and plastic (storage jars, coffee cups, glasses, mixing bowls, pitchers, coffeepots); stainless steel, aluminum, brushed nickel, and chrome (clock, pots and pans, lamps, coffee Thermos); black, white, or black and tan accents (china, linens, trays) and shots of red-orange (fresh flowers). Hide supplies or tools in other colors behind cabinet doors.

Place mats. Shop antiques stores for old school slates for use as table mats. Display them on an open shelf between meals to repeat the chalkboard theme.

Hanging shelves. To make a hanging shelf, *opposite,* buy one 3-inch-wide and one 5-inch-wide pine or birch board in the desired length (this shelf measures 8 feet long). For the hanging rail, screw the narrow board to one edge of the wider board. Attach the shelf to the wall through the front of the hanging rail, inserting screws at stud locations (check for studs with a stud finder). For the short shelf at the corner of the room, follow the same instructions.

Coffee bean storage. It's the old storage trick from the workbench in the garage. Instead of nails, nuts, and bolts, you'll be storing coffee beans (or other goodies). While shopping for groceries, choose spaghetti sauces in appealing screw-top containers; then recycle the jars for storage. If the screw-top lids clash with the color palette, spray them with silver metallic paint. Screw the lids to the underside of the wood shelf, allowing enough room between them for easy access. To keep track of a variety of coffee beans, use your computer to print labels on white paper. Cut out the labels and take them to a print shop for lamination. After they're laminated, trim the labels on a paper cutter, leaving a $\frac{1}{2}$-inch margin around the paper edges. With a paper punch, cut holes at the ends of the labels and thread them on kitchen string. Tie the kitchen string around the necks of the storage jars.

Artwork. To add coffee-shop atmosphere to the dining bar area, hang a wall art canvas of stacked dishes. Decorate the blackboard with the names of the coffee varieties you have in stock—items that can be "ordered" from your kitchen. Hang a pendant over the tabletop for a warm pool of light.

New white appliances, countertops, and backsplash tiles brighten a remodeled kitchen. Underfoot, new vinyl flooring has the look of real brick, setting the tone for a cottage theme.

COTTAGE KITCHEN

 BackGround

WALL, TRIM, AND CEILING COLOR white

WINDOW AND DOOR FRAMES painted to match cabinets

FLOOR COVERING vinyl flooring in brick design

FIXED LIGHTING recessed lighting

 Furniture

FIXED built-in cupboards with ceramic

countertops/backsplashes

FREESTANDING trestle table; bench; Windsor chairs

 accessories

MOOD LIGHTING French-style chandelier

TABLEWARE white ware and yellow ware

FABRICS white, red, and yellow fabrics

VINTAGE TOUCHES pine containers; country bottles

A fresh coat of paint is a cost-effective way to dress up a weary kitchen. A little prep work will make the job last: First, determine which type of paint is on the cabinets. Put rubbing alcohol on a clean rag and wipe an inside surface. If the paint comes up, it's latex (water-base); if the paint is unaffected, it's alkyd (oil-base). You can paint oil over latex; however, only certain latex paints will adhere to oils, so check the label before you buy paint. Thoroughly clean cabinets to remove dirt and cooking grease residue. Trisodium phosphate (TSP) is a popular cleaning agent. If you're replacing hardware, patch the old holes first. Lightly sand the surface and prime it to help the new paint adhere. Paint walls, moldings, ceiling, and window mullions white; paint cabinetry, door frames, and window frames dark green. Replace the hardware and add gathered valance to the top of the kitchen-sink window.

Arrange the furniture in the dining area, leaving enough space for traffic to pass by the table and through the French doors at the side of the room.

Hang a chandelier over the table. To dress it up, purchase a small shade-covering kit from a fabric or crafts supply store and decorate the tiny lampshades with yellow miniprint fabric. Install a dimmer switch for total control over lighting and atmosphere. Also, arrange the hanging chain so the chandelier can be lowered for a more intimate dining mood. Keep surfaces free of clutter, using food in plain containers as the only eye candy in the room.

A countrified chandelier, dressed in fabric-covered shades, gives a space instant character and calls attention to the luxurious volume of a vaulted ceiling.

Battens applied over flat walls increase cottage charm and layer a room with texture and visual interest.

A satisfying choice, brick-look vinyl flooring walks the cottage walk, talks the cottage talk, and cleans up well at the end of the day.

Food for thought...

Some paints are designed to stand up to the moisture and temperature changes in kitchens and baths. These usually cost a little more but are worth the expense. A smooth paint finish makes kitchen cleanup easier; eggshell and semigloss paints fit the bill, without generating excess shine.

Glass replaces wood panels in upper cabinet doors, creating a showcase for treasured china.

At night and on cloudy days, an over-the-sink pendant provides task lighting.

Paint interiors of open-view cupboards red to create a dramatic backdrop for dishware.

Bun feet, tucked into the toe-kick gap below base cabinets, create the illusion of freestanding furniture. Wood rectangles were glued onto the feet for a custom look.

Clever additions make basic fixed cabinets look like elegant freestanding furniture. A red-and-white color scheme speaks fluent Swedish.

Taste of sweden

Background

WALL AND TRIM COLOR white

WINDOW COVERINGS red and white toile cafe curtains

FLOOR COVERING pale wood laminate

Furniture

FIXED standard white cabinetry; countertops

FREESTANDING red stool(s)

accessories

LIGHTING pendent fixture; strip lights

EYE CANDY red and white china display; brushed-chrome hardware; red flowers

Before painting the walls, trim, and cabinetry, make additions to the cupboards. To create a hutch, find three elements at a home center that will bridge the gap between a set of upper and lower cabinets: a bead-board backsplash, an arched fascia (installed below the upper cabinet), and curved side brackets. On the upper doors, replace wood panels with glass and cut wood mullions (also purchased from a home center) to fit atop the glass. Glue the mullions to the door frames. Purchase bun feet and tuck them into the toe-kick gap, using glue to secure their positions. Paint the entire background and fixed cabinetry white except for the open-view cupboards. Paint the interior of open-view cupboards red. Add strip lights (available in hardware stores) on the underside of the upper cabinet to accent the display on the counter. Hang red and white toile curtains in the windows on white tension rods.

Paint counter stools. Red high-gloss latex enamel stands out. Arrange them around a bar-height table or along a counter.

Arrange red and white dishware in the open-view cupboards. Settle a few special pieces on the counter. An easel or a dab of tacky wax on the countertop will keep a large platter from slipping down from its display position and crashing on the floor.

Like the functioning center of any home, this kitchen is hardworking. Its retro style comes from basic building materials—wood, wood laminate, corrugated tin, metal, and glass—all without embellishment.

UTILITY CHIC

 ## Background

WALL AND CEILING COLOR cornsilk yellow

FLOORING wood laminate in a light maple color

FIXED LIGHTING recessed lighting; stainless-steel pendants

 ## Furniture

FIXED built-in cabinetry; appliances; island

FREESTANDING wood and stainless-steel bar-height chairs; classic modern refrigerator

 ## accessories

TABLEWARE glass; metal; ceramic dishware

RETRO TOUCHES '50s- and '60s-look ceramic vases; clear glass cylinders

Hire a carpenter and builder to install modern maple cabinetry, windows, flooring, new appliances, and a kitchen island (you may need an architect to draw plans before you begin). The creative part of building your background is choosing materials in their purest states. Keep your focus on classic and timeless materials, picturing them in present-day, cutting-edge design. Use this photograph as your starting point and translate it to the space you have. Once the floors, walls, fixed cupboards, and built-in appliances are in, you'll need to consider surface finishes: clear varnishes for wood, eggshell-finish paint for walls, and rice-paper glass inserts for cupboard doors.

New retro-style bar-height chairs slide under the kitchen island counter. If possible, incorporate an old appliance, such as the refrigerator shown here, into the kitchen design. Mixing old with new is a fun challenge for your design eye.

Collect retro ceramic vases and use them as eye-catching accents to highlight a surface or two—no more. Retro is clean and uncluttered, so keep accessories to a minimum. Find new, retro-style dishes for tabletop use. When choosing linens and fabrics for the kitchen, keep their colors neutral and natural. For an occasional splash of natural color, choose clean-lined long-stemmed blooms without soft leaves and fluffy textures. Stand the flowers upright in a clear glass cylinder or glass block to show off the strong lines of both.

A 40-year-old refrigerator is a vintage modern accent.

Line open-view cupboard doors with glass made with the look of rice paper to help screen the clutter of dishes inside.

Any mess on the cooktop hides behind the raised eating counter.

A modern angular island is clad with corrugated tin—a salvaged roofing material.

Maple-color wood laminate, chosen to reinforce the design in the rest of the home, is a durable, low-cost flooring option.

A standard cupboard without its doors becomes a showcase for dishware and allows easy removal and return of everyday items.

A custom countertop, ordered without a back lip, blends seamlessly with a new backsplash.

Food for thought...

Evaluate your storage: Are related items grouped together? Are small appliances positioned close to the countertop where you use them? Do you keep the items you use most frequently near the front of a cabinet or drawer? Could you benefit from pullout shelves? A little planning will maximize your space and make your kitchen tasks more enjoyable.

To streamline your kitchen and give it a modern look, remove the window cornice and a few cabinet doors from standard cupboards.

sleek & svelte

 Background

WALL AND CABINET COLORS white; pale blue-green

WINDOW COVERINGS silver-metallic venetian blinds

FLOOR COVERING pale oak wood laminate

FIXED LIGHTING overhead fixtures

 Furniture

FIXED upper and lower cabinets

FREESTANDING rolling work island

 accessories

TASK LIGHTING metallic pendant

TABLEWARE gray and white china; plain glasses

STYLISH TOUCHES mesh baskets; oversize green-glass

vessels; undersink curtain panel

Remove doors from inexpensive cabinets and replace a standard window cornice with a simple shelf. Paint all wood surfaces with an energizing coat of white paint, using a semigloss finish for bright, fresh, washable surfaces. Top the newly painted lower cabinets with white countertops and a white ceramic-tile backsplash. Accent the backsplash with small, shiny tiles attached with tile adhesive. Cover the surrounding walls in soft blue-green, eggshell-finish latex paint. Paint all moldings and trim in the same white as the cabinetry. For a flash of silver, slip inside-mount, metallic-finish blinds in the windows. Add more sparkle by installing brushed-chrome hardware on the base cabinets and an arched chrome faucet at the sink.

Assemble a rolling table, purchased from a discount store in a flat-pack carton. Place it in an open space at one end of the kitchen or between counters as an island for extra work space and storage. Another option for a rolling cart is a "pantry"—a tall cabinet with storage shelves and baskets for food and supplies.

Arrange showcase dishware in the open upper cupboard (adjust cabinet shelves, if possible, to fit tall and short pieces). Settle a large gray serving tray along the back wall as an accent piece within the dishware arrangement. Add glass vessels to the countertop. For the curtain panel below the sink, use tension bolts to hang a steel cable wire between the sides of the opening. Slip clip-on rings over the wire and clip a white cotton curtain panel to the rings.

If you're an avid recipe collector who enjoys cooking and hosting large gatherings, your kitchen needs a library for cookbooks, magazines, entertaining ideas, and party menus.

room for recipes

 BACKGROUND

WALL, FIXED CABINETRY AND TILE COLORS black; white; red

WINDOW COVERINGS white venetian blinds

FLOOR COVERING wood planking

FIXED LIGHTING recessed lighting

 Furniture

FIXED built-in cabinets; island; counter dining unit;

appliances; sink

FREESTANDING black metal counter stools

 accessories

TASK LIGHTING undercabinet and over-the-stove lighting

TABLEWARE black, white, and red dishes

ACCENTS red flowers; food; table linens

In a large black and white kitchen such as this one, remove two cupboard doors on one or two walls to reveal the shelf space behind them. Paint the back wall(s) of the cupboard in a striking color (red is a great accent for a black and white color scheme). This creates a welcome background break, interrupting the steady rhythm of closed cabinet doors. It also makes a striking backdrop for a display of dishes or a special collection of teapots.

Furnishings. Abundant cabinet and counter space, two cleanup centers, appliances, a six-burner range, and an island library make this kitchen "action central" for a family that loves to cook and entertain. Because much of the furniture is fixed or built in, few freestanding pieces are needed. Slide three black metal bar-height chairs under the raised counter, and you're ready to eat.

Accent with red. It's tempting to clutter vast counter spaces with everything you want to keep handy. However, this decorating recipe calls for good editing. Limit countertop accessorizing to black and white items. Toss in strategically placed red accents to punch up the neutral scheme. Red hand towels and trays, red-top cannisters, and red fruit and flowers break up the monotony of broad black and white surfaces.

The island holds family recipes and reference materials for planning meals and parties. Pasteboard file boxes on the lower shelf keep cooking magazines indexed according to title.

A few open cupboards reveal their contents, relieving the tedium of so many closed doors.

Three spacious compartments, each with a center shelf, organize the kitchen library.

Hook-and-loop tape holds a framed print on backsplash tile.

Small spaces and small budgets usually go hand in hand. Follow this penny-wise recipe for packing a tiny apartment kitchen with personality and space-saving pieces.

comfort sweet

background

WALL AND CABINET COLORS olive; gold; white

WINDOW COVERINGS venetian blinds with wood blades

FLOOR COVERINGS wood planking; braided rug

FIXED LIGHTING ceiling light

Furniture

FIXED built-in cupboards; refrigerator; sink; cooktop

FREESTANDING antique wood table; antique wood chairs

accessories

MOOD AND TASK LIGHTING countertop and tabletop lamps

TABLEWARE antique black and white transferware

VINTAGE TOUCHES salvaged antique pediment; clock; painted trays; framed book illustrations

For the background ingredient, paint the walls above a white tile backsplash an olive green (purchase wall paint in an eggshell finish for subtle sheen and washability). Select two gold semigloss paints from the same paint-color strip for the cabinets. Paint the cabinet units with the darker gold and the cabinet doors with the lighter tone. Paint window frames and moldings in a high-gloss white. Hang inside-mount wood blinds in the windows. Give flat-front cabinets character by choosing inexpensive prints from a book. Put them in plain black frames from a discount store. Predrill holes in the sides of the frames through the cabinet doors. Then secure the frames with black drywall screws. For extra character and personality, position an architectural pediment in the niche above the upper cabinetry.

Shed some light. Arrange a small table and chairs parallel to the kitchen counter. Put one end of the table against a wall that offers easy access to an electrical outlet. Place a tall, attractive lamp on the table so it can pour light gently over the table surface like a chandelier. This arrangement makes it possible to plug in the lamp. Settle a tiny lamp on the counter to light kitchen tasks.

Adorn the niche above the upper cabinetry. A clock is one of the most important items in a kitchen. Add off-beat combinations of your favorite pieces, such as a sculpted pig next to a delicate Grecian-style pitcher.

BED
rooms

In contrast to the active ways of the cooking, eating, work, and bath areas of your home, measure your bedroom with a different set of values. At its best, your bedroom gives you complete privacy and tranquility, and expresses your personal tastes. To create bedroom style that's all your own, read this chapter for inspiration. The first part of the chapter reveals the decorating layers of this lavender retreat. The rest of the chapter offers a menu of bedrooms to please your palette.

You spend about a third of your life sleeping—a practical reason for buying a good bed. Your bed is also a place of dreams and plans, and comfort in sickness and health. Read the recipe for this restful getaway on the next few pages.

lavender retreat

 1 BACKGROUND

WALL AND TRIM COLORS corn silk yellow; white paint; lavender and white striped wallcovering

FLOOR COVERINGS white-painted subflooring; flokati rug

 2 Furniture

BED mattress; box spring; metal frame; wallpapered headboard

SEATING rattan chairs

STORAGE bedside chests; tall chests

 3 accessories

MOOD AND TASK LIGHTING bedside lamps; floor lamp

PERSONAL COMFORTS quilts; pillows; decorative cushions; family photographs

CONVENIENCES clock; water carafe; mirrors

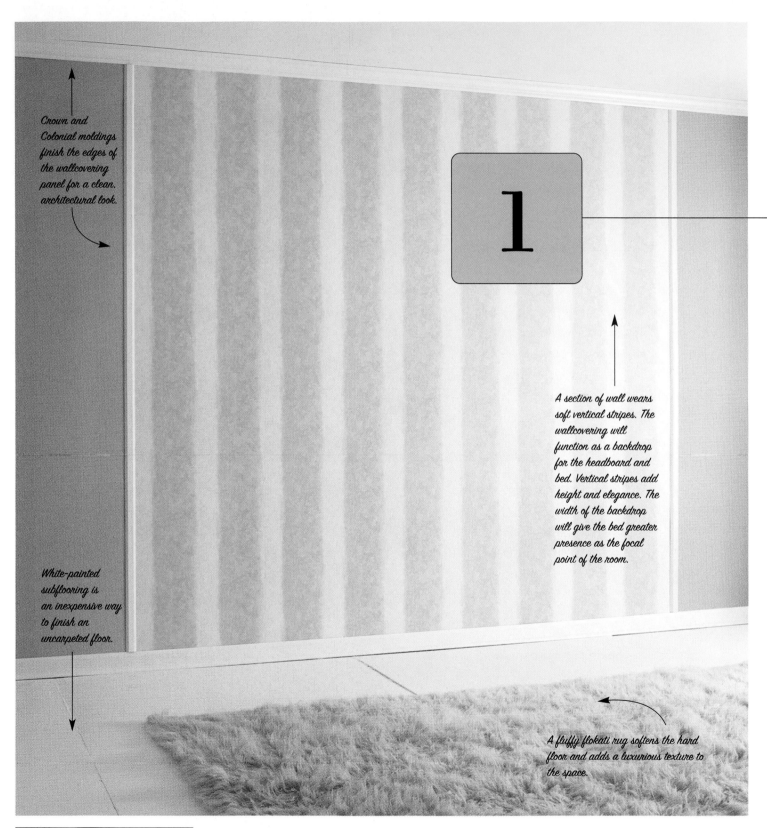

Crown and Colonial moldings finish the edges of the wallcovering panel for a clean, architectural look.

White-painted subflooring is an inexpensive way to finish an uncarpeted floor.

1

A section of wall wears soft vertical stripes. The wallcovering will function as a backdrop for the headboard and bed. Vertical stripes add height and elegance. The width of the backdrop will give the bed greater presence as the focal point of the room.

A fluffy flokati rug softens the hard floor and adds a luxurious texture to the space.

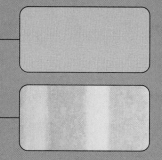

WALLS Wall colors control the mood of a bedroom. Periwinkle blue—a violet blue—takes a sleeping zone toward a meditative attitude. Yellow, when it is pale and sunny, lifts your mood in the morning. However, choosing the right yellow for a bedroom requires careful consideration. Remember that a sunny yellow on a paint chip triples in brightness after you put it on the wall. Avoid lemon yellows with too much zing and zest for a bedroom.

B a c K G r o u n D Sometimes a patterned fabric or wallcovering generates the overall design of a room. Three coordinating wallcoverings—one on a plain wall; the other two on furniture pieces—in this room pull plain white surfaces into sharp focus.

Create a backdrop for your bed—and make it a focal point—by hanging several wallcovering panels on the wall that will harbor the bed. Make the entire section as wide as the width of the bed plus two bedside chests plus 12 inches. Paint the remaining walls pale corn silk yellow. Add white crown and base moldings. Cover the seams where the wallpapered and painted sections join with white-painted Colonial or library moldings (see detail, *right*).

For chic but inexpensive flooring in a carpetless room, paint the floorboards or subflooring with white high-gloss floor-and-deck paint. Choose a latex enamel that you can easily wash and touch-up. Coat the floor two or three times for durability. (Use multiple coats of paint instead of a polyurethane sealant, which limits your cleaning and repainting options.) After allowing the paint to cure for two days, position a large flokati area rug in the space where the bed will be, so its soft texture greets your feet when you get up each day.

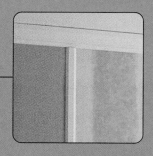

WOODWORK White moldings add crisp architecture to a room. If you cut your own moldings, paint them before attaching them to the ceiling, wall, or floor.

FLOOR COVERINGS Contrasting textures feel good underfoot. Here, a furry white area rug warms up hard flooring while preserving the light look of the room.

F u r n i t u r e In this bedroom, ordinary fiberboard and white storage pieces get facelifts—masks made out of wallcovering. Two patterned coverings—a floral design and a grid design—coordinate with the wallcovering applied to the wall during the background stage of decorating *(previous page)*.

To make the headboard panels, buy two 4×8-foot panels of medium-density fiberboard (also known as MDF). Ask the home center where you make the purchase to cut two panels 9 inches wide and three panels 16 inches wide for a double or queen-size bed. (For a king-size bed, adjust the widths.) Working on a large, flat surface, cover the fronts, sides, and ends of the panels with wallcovering. Measure and cut the wallcovering long and wide enough to securely wrap around the sides to the backs of the panels. If pattern repeat is obvious, match the design from panel to panel (this will require making some allowances in your measurements). Run each wallcovering panel through a wallcovering water trough to get it wet, working only one prepasted panel at a time. "Book" the panel for five minutes (fold it back on itself sticky sides together) to ready the paste. Then apply the covering over the fiberboard panel, keeping the design square with the edges of the panel. Wipe away excess water and paste with a sponge. At the sides and ends, wrap the fiberboard snugly, like a gift box. Being careful not to cut too much, snip away excess wallcovering at corners for a cleaner wrap. Lay the panel flat on its back to dry. Repeat the procedure for the remaining panels, alternating the designs and widths.

To decorate drawer fronts, wrap them like the headboard panels, following the steps, *above*.

Two matching chests of drawers—one for him and one for her—get the same decorative treatment as the headboard panels.

Matching chairs—one for him and one for her—turn one end of the bedroom into an after-hours sitting area.

Substitutions: after-hours comfort

Lightweight garden chairs may not offer the cushiony comfort you seek in a bedroom. In that case, consider a pair of upholstered armchairs, a love seat, or a long settee. In a bedroom with plenty of space (most bedrooms in newer homes are large), create a seating group around a coffee table—for example, a generous armchair and a long upholstered chaise with an adjustable end. Arrange the seating pieces in an L-shape around the coffee table, facing the group toward the bed.

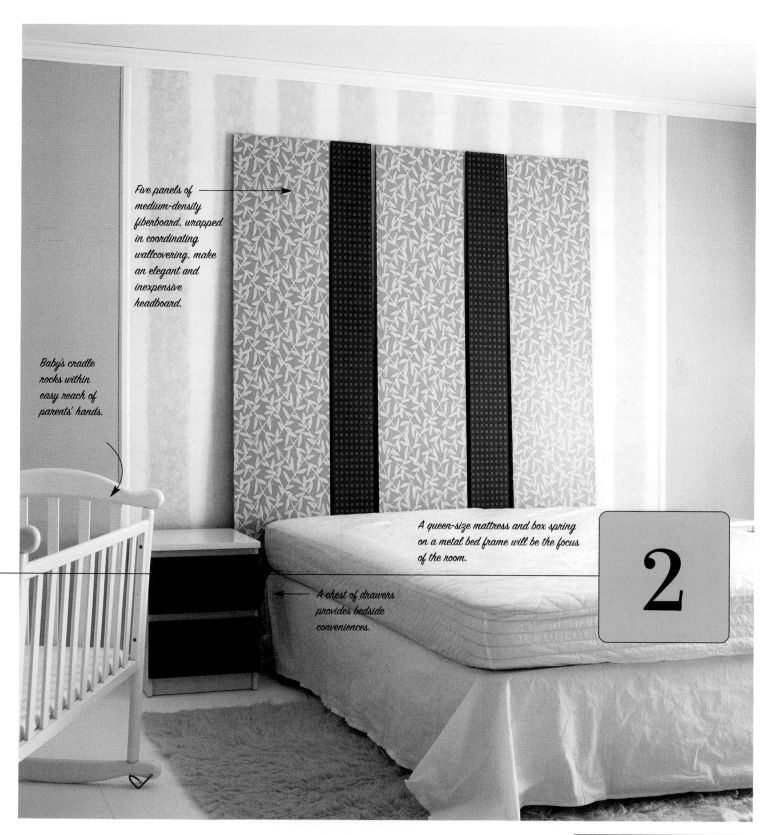

Five panels of medium-density fiberboard, wrapped in coordinating wallcovering, make an elegant and inexpensive headboard.

Baby's cradle rocks within easy reach of parents' hands.

A queen-size mattress and box spring on a metal bed frame will be the focus of the room.

A chest of drawers provides bedside conveniences.

2

Close-to-the-skin comforts are essential in a bedroom recipe.

Only a few key items belong on a bedside table. Clutter chases away bedroom calm.

3

Precious metals and fragrant linen waters add a sensuous dimension to the dressing area.

accessories. You deserve sparkle and personal comforts that please the senses.

Lighting. Lamps near each side of the bed make reading and working in bed convenient. Typically, nightstand lamps are shorter than traditional table lamps to allow for reclining while you read. Place the bottom of the shade at about cheek height so the glare of the bulb doesn't cause eyestrain. Flared lamp shades help direct light toward the bed and your reading material. Arrange lamps so you can turn them off without getting out of bed. As long as they complement each other, bedside lamp styles need not match exactly. Choose fixtures of roughly the same height or purchase matching shades to link them. Elsewhere in the room, especially near a seating area, add lamplight to lift the shadows from a dark corner and light a nearby mirror.

Mirrors. If you dress in your bedroom, fasten a full-length mirror to the front of a closet door or to a wall near a chest of drawers. On top of the chest, add an old-fashioned magnifying mirror or a newer model with built-in lighting. For maximum clarity and style, choose plain round, oval, or rectangular mirrors rather than frosted-glass mirrors or mirrors etched with motifs. Plain mirrors will blend well with lighting fixtures of any style.

Cushions and comforters pamper the body and soothe the spirit. While searching through the wallcovering books during the background phase of this project, check to see if any of the coordinating designs are also offered in fabrics. Order 2- or 3-yard lengths to sew into knife- or piped-edge pillows or cushions for seating. To sew knife-edge pillows, buy 20-inch-square down pillow forms from a textiles store. From the fabric, cut two 22-inch squares for each pillow. Using $\frac{1}{2}$-inch seam allowances, machine-sew the pillow front and back together, right sides facing. On one edge, leave an 8-inch opening for turning the pillow cover right side out and stuffing the pillow form inside. Once the form is inside the cover, fluff the pillow to fill the corners. Handstitch to close the opening.

An uplight floor lamp lights shadowy corners at the top of the room and adds a vertical line to balance low-slung seating pieces.

To create a restful retreat in precious little floor space, combine basic geometry with crisp white walls and curtains. Then slip away to sleep.

SO SOOTHING

 1   BACKGROUND

WALL COLORS white; celadon green

WINDOW COVERINGS sheer white panels

FLOOR COVERING wall-to-wall taupe carpet

FIXED LIGHTING ceiling fan light fixture

 2   FURNITURE

BED mattress; box spring; metal frame

TABLES bedside table

STORAGE chest of drawers

 3   accessories

MOOD LIGHTING bedside lamps

PERSONAL COMFORTS bed skirt; duvet; duvet cover; pillows; framed photos; art

NATURAL TOUCH a palm leaf from a large outdoor plant

Color. Paint walls and woodwork with a clean, bright white paint—eggshell finish for walls and enamel for woodwork. For the floor-to-ceiling faux headboard, measure the width of the bed and mark the same width on the wall where the bed will be placed; the lines you draw indicate the sides of the faux headboard. Use a level to ensure that the lines are plumb. With painter's tape, mask off the vertical lines, the base molding, and the ceiling. Paint the headboard panel celadon green; remove the tape. Hang plain white cotton curtain panels at the window.

Move the bed into place in front of the painted panel. Add a chest of drawers and a bedside table for storage.

Dress the bed with a white tailored or pleated bed skirt (remove the mattress, fit the skirt over the box spring, and replace the mattress). Cover the mattress with a mattress pad; add a fitted sheet. Slip a geometric-design duvet cover over a down duvet (no need for a top sheet with a washable duvet) and fluff it over the bed. Layer on two sets of pillows. Set lamps on both bedside surfaces, for reading light and for mood. Hang pictures, if desired. To give the room a modest burst of energy, cut a branch from a palm or evergreen and place it in a vase at one side of the bed.

A painted vertical swath of celadon green behind the bed creates the illusion of a more voluminous space.

Cool tones create a restful room.

A single giant palm leaf, cut from an outdoor plant, makes quick, dramatic artwork.

Use streamlined motifs—stripes, squares, and ovals—on bedding. Timeless shapes create a contemporary clean look.

Bedding with a large-scale geometric print makes a small room look bigger than it really is.

An offbeat
marriage of a
birdcage stand
and a fancy
chandelier join
together as
a bedside
floorlamp.

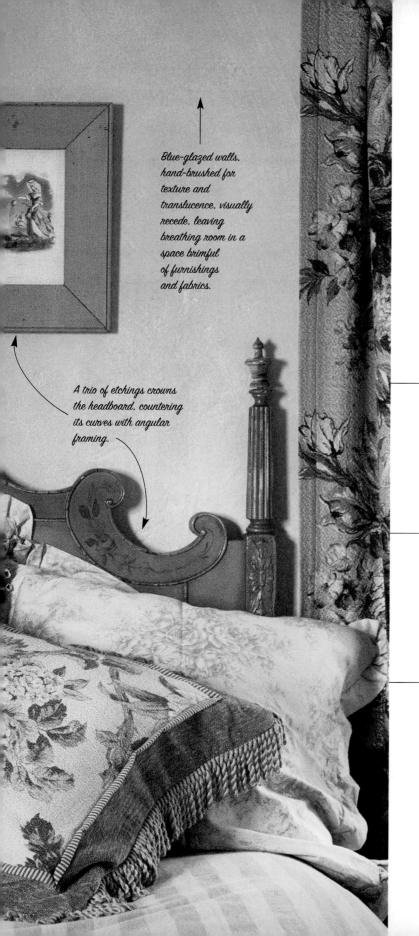

Blue-glazed walls, hand-brushed for texture and translucence, visually recede, leaving breathing room in a space brimful of furnishings and fabrics.

A trio of etchings crowns the headboard, countering its curves with angular framing.

Two elements—the well-worn and the well-preserved—come together in a delicious and original concoction of beauty and wear.

HOLLYWOOD CHIC

1 BACKGROUND

WALL COLOR soft, streaked blue glaze

WINDOW COVERINGS vintage floral panels

FLOOR COVERINGS carpeting; bedside tapestry rugs

2 Furniture

BED 1940s French-style bed

TABLE antique wicker bedside table

STORAGE antique chest of drawers

3 accessories

MOOD LIGHTING birdcage chandelier; antique lamp

PERSONAL COMFORTS matte/shiny striped duvet cover;

down duvet; ruffled pillows; floral cushions

VINTAGE TOUCHES clock collection; giant mirror; etchings

A mirror framed in dark wood spans a major part of one wall, making the small room appear almost twice its actual size.

A clock collection is a personal indulgence arranged to amuse.

Overscale furniture makes a small room seem cozy.

Glaze the walls. Blue paint and decorator's glaze make the ordinary extraordinary. If you're a beginner at glazing walls, purchase a glaze kit complete with instructions at a paint supply store. These walls were hand-brushed in a crosshatch technique to give them texture and translucence. For window treatments, slip ivory sheers on tension rods and mount them inside the window frames. For beauty, hang side curtain panels fashioned from vintage floral fabric; install them on outside-mount metal rods 3 inches above the window frame. Install a Hollywood-size mirror on the wall to make a small room appear larger-than-life, brimming with luxury and glamour.

Feature the bed. Make it the focal point of the room. Invest in a good mattress and box spring and scout up an antique headboard that makes you feel like a movie star. Position the bed so that the headboard faces the doorway. (It's *feng shui* to be able to view the door from your bed.) If you need more storage than your closet allows, buy chests of drawers.

"Prop" the room. Using pieces that delight your sensibilities, weave fragments of your personality into the bedroom story. Add a bedside lamp for reading and a floorlamp for drama. Make the room bloom with vintage floral fabrics on bed cushions. Then sweeten the space with delicate flowers that grow in garden pots near a window.

SET THE SCENE For storybook charm right out of an old romantic movie, create a soft backdrop of smoky lavender-blue walls, floral draperies at the windows, and a giant mirror that doubles the size of the room and reflects the whole scene.

ADD FURNITURE The central focus in a bedroom is the bed; storage for clothing is also key. If you have built-in closets, the only true necessity is a wonderful bed. However, a bedside table is convenient for storing jewelry and displaying personal props.

ADD CHARACTER with older, distressed items, collecting display ideas from antiques stores or old Hollywood movies. For example, some antiques vendors display chandeliers in birdcage stands—a nostalgic idea to romance your bedroom. If you're a clock-watcher, mass them together for collective appeal.

Floor-to-ceiling curtains add more grace to the windows and give the bed the look of a four-poster.

A candle chandelier is less expensive than an electric one—and more magical.

Install molding around the bed curtains and above the windows to add architectural interest and to conceal curtain hardware.

Fabric creates drama while filling voluminous space.

When the decorating challenges of a spacious master suite overwhelm a small budget, flood the room with fabric to achieve a soft cocoon.

FLORAL OASIS

 1 BACKGROUND

WALL AND TRIM COLORS beige; white

WINDOW COVERINGS floor-to-ceiling fabric panels

FLOOR COVERING carpeting

FIXED LIGHTING recessed lighting

 2 FURNITURE

BED mattress and box spring

TABLE distressed-white bedside table

 3 accessories

MOOD LIGHTING candle chandelier

PERSONAL COMFORTS down duvet; bed curtains; pillows and cushions; bed throw

EYE CANDY curtains; photos; flowers; carved mirror

Paint the walls beige and coat the base moldings and window frames in a bright white enamel. For the chair rail, cut enough lengths of library molding to fit around the entire room. Paint them white before attaching them to the walls at a 36-inch height. Dress the windows with wood-molding cornices and floral fabric panels (staple the fabric inside the cornices before attaching the cornices to the wall).

Place the mattress and box spring against a wall. From 1-inch-thick plywood, cut a headboard 6 inches wider than the bed and 48 inches high (plywood usually comes in 4×8-foot sheets). Cover the plywood frame for the headboard with batting and a layer of plain, deep beige fabric, stapling the raw edges to the back of the plywood. Screw the headboard to the wall at the desired height behind the bed. Then frame it with fluted white-painted molding. To build the bed-curtain frame, install white-painted molding on the ceiling directly above the bed (see detail, *opposite, left*). Bring bedside tables into position and place a writing desk at an angle in a corner of the room (diagonally placed furnishings take up more space and energize a room).

Staple bed-curtain panels to the inside of the white frame attached to the ceiling over the bed. Sew a duvet cover from matching floral fabric; sew matching ruffled pillow covers for Euro-square pillows. Then layer on decorative pillows for a lush look. Hang a carved mirror at the side of the bed and suspend a candle chandelier from the ceiling over the center of the bed.

Plant a field of stenciled flowers above the bed;
then scatter a few more across the ceiling for
your own little upside-down garden.

UPSY DAISY

1   B A C K G R O U N D

WALL COLORS green; blue; white; flower colors

WINDOW COVERINGS sheer white panels

FLOOR COVERING wood laminate flooring

FIXED LIGHTING ceiling fixture

2   F u r n i t u r e

BED mattress; box spring; metal frame

TABLES white bedside table; decorator table

STORAGE white chests of drawers

3   a c c e s s o r i e s

TASK LIGHTING swing-arm lamps

PERSONAL COMFORTS dust ruffle; down duvet; floral linens; flowers

CONVENIENCES phone; clock

On the accent wall where the bed will be placed, use painter's tape to mask off a headboard panel 2 inches wider than the bed on each side. Paint this headboard section red; remove the tape. Retape and paint the rest of the wall blue on each side of the headboard panel. Paint the three remaining walls white. Create a crackle finish by applying premixed crackle medium (available at crafts, home decorating, and paint stores) to the entire wall according to the manufacturer's directions. Using a ragging mitt, add a top coat of light-green paint to the entire wall. (Dip the mitt into the paint; then blot it onto kraft paper or scrap wood to remove the excess.) Gently press the paint over the crackle medium, reloading the mitt as needed. Apply the top coat evenly, and avoid layering which could lift off the crackle medium. For the flowers, choose a single flower stencil that imitates the shape and size of the flowers on your bed linens. Purchase stencil paints that match the bed linen colors. Following the directions on the stencil paint labels, stencil your design over the crackled area of the walls and across the ceiling. Hang swing-arm lamps on either side of the stenciled headboard panel.

Place a mattress and box spring on a metal bed frame and roll the bed into place in front of the headboard wall. Add bedside tables and chests of drawers as needed.

Dress the bed with a white dust ruffle and the floral-printed bedding that inspired the headboard wall. Cover the decorator table with matching fabric. Place bedside comforts and conveniences on the tabletops.

Stencils echoing the pattern in the linens scatter over a crackled surface. A few more drift up the wall and across the ceiling.

Swing-arm lamps, hung on each side of the stenciled headboard panel, invite reading in bed.

Bed linens inspire the wall design.

Stencil by using a pouncing motion to push paint through openings in a floral pattern, *top*. Sprinkle the same motif over the wall at various intervals, *above*.

Cherry red walls welcome guests with warmth and depth.

A tattered armchair gains casual elegance with an unfitted slipcover of creamy cotton duck fabric.

A tall oak chest of drawers is a family heirloom that brings a story to the room.

To make a guest bedroom inviting, choose a cherry hue for the walls. The warm color creates a cozy atmosphere and makes white woodwork stand out.

Guest Quarters

1 BACKGROUND

WALL AND TRIM COLORS cherry red; white

WINDOW COVERINGS white half-shutters

FLOOR COVERING carpeting

FIXED LIGHTING ceiling fixture

2 FURNITURE

BED oak bed frame; mattress; box spring

SEATING corner armchair

STORAGE tall oak chest; bedside chests; radiator ledge

3 accessories

MOOD LIGHTING bedside and chairside table lamps

PERSONAL COMFORTS quilt; needlepoint pillows

VINTAGE TOUCH antique European poster

NATURAL TOUCH fresh flowers from the garden

Before redecorating a small guest room, such as the one shown here, clear the room of furniture and accessories to make it easier to move about with a painting ladder. Mask off the woodwork to paint the walls cherry red. Let the walls dry for 24 hours before masking them off to paint the woodwork in a high-gloss white. (If you prefer, do the work in reverse order, painting the woodwork first and finishing with the walls.) Purchase shutters to fit the lower halves of double-hung windows. Paint or spray them in the same high-gloss white as the woodwork before attaching them to the window frames with hinges.

Rearrange the furniture so that a focal point piece catches the eye as guests enter this charming sanctuary. For example, the tall oak chest of drawers, *opposite*, a family heirloom, settles snugly between two windows facing the entrance to the room. The head of the bed is placed against the only plain wall in the room. Then an old armchair is brought back into the room to sit in the last empty corner. With a shelf laid across its top, the radiator becomes a chairside table.

Accessorize to make an old-fashioned sleepover for guests to remember. That means old-fashioned textiles: a loose throw and a pretty needlepoint pillow to dress up the chair, a quilt and matelassé pillows for the bed. Add a few graphic elements—framed photographs, an advertising poster, and a pair of cranberry-glass lamps to complement the luxurious red walls. Shortly before guests arrive, arrange fresh flowers on top of a chest of drawers.

Despite its hard-core industrial image, steel cable has plenty of decorating potential. Here, industrial meets antique in a chic eclectic mix.

cable Haven

 1 **B a c k g r o u n d**

WALL AND TRIM COLOR creamy white

FLOOR COVERINGS wood laminate

FIXED LIGHTING cable lighting

 2 **F u r n i t u r e**

BED mattress; box spring; metal frame; cable bedposts

SEATING a pair of metal dining chairs

STORAGE antique pie safe; antique chest; bedside chest

 3 **a c c e s s o r i e s**

PERSONAL COMFORTS down-filled duvet; pillows; bed curtains; towels

VINTAGE TOUCHES antique bracket decoration; books

NATURAL TOUCHES pine cones; fresh flowers

Create faux paneling. Install 1½-inch-wide lattice strips to drywall at 12-inch intervals. Paint the walls and ceiling in a creamy white, satin finish paint. (Leave an antique window frame natural). Hang cable lighting near the ceiling. (Follow manufacturer's directions.)

Make a four-poster bed. Use a screw eye to secure a 2-inch hitching ring to a wall stud on each side of the bed (see the detail above, *opposite*). If you don't have conveniently located studs, attach hitching ring to the floor. Attach screw eyes to ceiling joists above the head and foot of the bed. On the floor at the foot of the bed, secure two flat-base screw eyes (see detail below, *opposite*), one on each side. Add a hitching ring. Attach steel cables at the head of the bed first. Use thimbles to make neat loops secured by ferrules. Thread the cable through the ceiling-mounted screw eyes. Create loops at the ends of the cable and attach it to the floor with turnbuckles and S-hooks, also shown in the detail below, *opposite*. Tighten the turnbuckles. Move in the bed and storage pieces.

Accessorize by hanging floral curtain panels from the cable near the head of the bed (use metal clip rings). Dress the bed, fill the storage pieces, and add a tray for books at the foot of the bed. Decorate the top of the pie safe with baskets of pine cones and flowers.

Cable lighting puts old-fashioned furnishings in a modern light.

A cable canopy holds a pair of vintage bedside curtains that draws closed for cozy sleeping quarters.

Lattice strips, placed every 12 inches over drywall, turn plain walls into paneled pretenders.

Attach cables at the ceiling first. Use thimbles to make neat loops secured by ferrules, *top.* Create loops at the bottom ends of the cables and attach them to the floor with turnbuckles and S-hooks, *bottom.*

Carefully trim
the panel
from behind
the window,
leaving a
½-inch margin.

At the head of the bed, an embroidered insert forms a fabric window that adds subtle texture and visually links the sheers to the natural hue of the matelassé spread.

Long panels of sheer fabric puddle slightly onto the floor.

Smooth, slick laminate wood flooring contrasts with the soft, delicate texture of the bed curtains.

Elegant embroidered panels hanging from long fabric ties surround a railed four-poster bed, enveloping it in a cloud of luxury.

sheer luxury

 1 **B a c k g r o u n d**

WALL AND TRIM COLORS pale lavender-blue; white

WINDOW COVERINGS sheer embroidered panels

FLOOR COVERING wood laminate

FIXED LIGHTING ceiling fixture

 2 **F u r n i t u r e**

BED black-metal four-poster

TABLE folding bedside tray

STORAGE white-painted chests of drawers

 3 **a c c e s s o r i e s**

MOOD LIGHTING white table lamp

PERSONAL COMFORTS pillows; sheets; matelassé bedcover

NATURAL TOUCH fresh flowers

Paint walls pale lavender-blue, a color that's as fragile as sheer embroidered fabric. Hang sheer curtain panels at the window using a black-metal rod to match the bed. **Position the poster bed** against the wall so that the headboard faces the entryway. Include storage chests and bedside trays.

Make two types of curtain panels. Place one set along the sides and foot of the bed, the other at the head of the bed. For the side and foot panels, cut lengths of embroidered fabric about 3 inches longer than the measurement from the bed rail to the floor. Using the full width of the fabric, cut enough pieces so that when pieced together they measure 1½ times the width of the bed. Narrowly hem each piece on all four sides, but do not join them. For ties, cut 16-inch ribbon strips. Fold in half crosswise and sew to the upper edge of the panels every 12 inches. For the headboard panel, join two lengths of fabric, using a French seam. Hem the edges. For the insert, cut a tightly embroidered piece of fabric 1 inch larger on all sides than the desired measurement. Press all edges under ½ inch, then another ½ inch to encase the raw edges. Position the insert on top of the headboard panel; pin. Topstitch it to the panel along the hemmed edges. Carefully trim the panel from behind the window, leaving a ½-inch margin (see detail, *opposite left*). Clip diagonally into the corners and roll the margin back to form a narrow hem and encase the raw edges. Sew the hem, using a slip stitch. Add ties and hang curtains on the bed. Bring in bedding, a lamp, and bedside comforts.

BaTH
rooms

Like kitchens, bathrooms come with water features and fixtures that must be integrated into decorating plans. Unless you completely remodel your bathroom, these pieces influence the overall style or look you plan. To see your bathroom in a new way, turn the pages of this chapter. You'll find the recipe for this sassy sauna-style space as well as ingredients for a romantic country getaway, a modern water world, and an eclectic redo. See which one appeals most to your bathing sensibilities.

For some people an efficient shower is the ultimate bathroom luxury. For others, it's a laid-back soak in the tub, where the body revels in silky waters and eases into relaxed oblivion. If you're part of the latter group, note this recipe for a private spa that comforts the body and spirit.

sauna STYLE

1 BACKGROUND

WALL COLORS lime green; avocado; licorice; pistachio

WOOD ELEMENTS cedar planking; sandblasted door

FLOOR COVERINGS slate ceramic tile; black throw rug

LIGHTING pendants; overhead recessed fixtures

2 FURNITURE

FIXED white pedestal sink; tub; toilet

FREESTANDING storage tower; hanging cupboard with bamboo insets; cane stool; bamboo basket; cedar shelf; towel ladder

3 accessories

MOOD LIGHTING candles set in stone

PERSONAL COMFORTS towels; weathered mirror; extendable mirror; small storage containers; full-length mirror

NATURAL TOUCHES stones; bamboo sticks

A light band at the top of the room maintains the spacious feeling. →

1

An accent strip between the two green walls defines the space and gives it a zap of energy.

Ceramic flooring, a smart choice for rooms with water, is best balanced with soft, fluffy rugs that comfort the soles of your feet and guard against slipping.

A slightly more intense green provides a fresh backdrop for white furniture and fixtures, accenting their clean-lined appeal.

BaCKGROUND Like most bathrooms about to be refurbished, this one began with fixed features: a pedestal sink, claw-foot tub, and standard toilet. Professionals installed a ceramic tile floor, cedar-clad tub surround, and an old sandblasted door. Unless you are a professional, hire the installation of these key bathroom elements to ensure stylish and functional results. Save for yourself the more enjoyable aspects, such as painting and choosing accessories.

To paint walls like these, you'll need three variations on the yellow-green color scheme—pale pistachio green, a slightly more intense darker pistachio, and a medium-dark avocado green (see samples, *above right*). Buy paint with a semigloss or high-gloss finish for easy cleaning and wipe-downs. With a level and pencil, mark a horizontal line on the walls around the entire room 72 inches from the floor. With painter's tape, mask off the top section of the wall. Paint it with the palest green and remove the tape. When the paint has dried 24 hours, mask off the bottom section and paint that section with the slightly darker pistachio color. Remove the tape and allow the paint to dry 24 hours. For the accent band, paint a 2-inch-wide strip with the avocado green. After it has dried 24 hours, apply two rows of painter's tape at the center of the strip, creating a tiny horizontal gap that's ½-inch wide. Fill the gap with black paint, using an artist's brush.

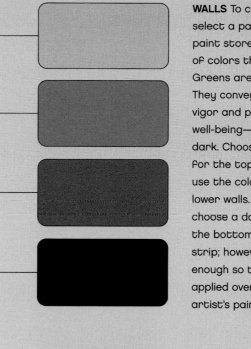

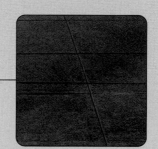

WALLS To choose wall colors, select a paint strip (available at paint stores) that contains a set of colors that appeal to you. Greens are easy to live with. They convey good health and vigor and promote a sense of well-being—if they're not too dark. Choose the lightest pastel for the top sections of the walls; use the color next to it for the lower walls. For the accent band, choose a dark green that's near the bottom of the same paint strip; however, keep it light enough so that the black stripe applied over it will show up. Use an artist's paint for the stripe.

TUB SURROUND A cedar-clad tub area is created with 8-inch cedar planking attached over studs. An inset shelf, built along the side of the tub, is backed with ceramic tile that matches the floor.

FLOOR COVERINGS Perfect for the bathroom, a waterproof, stain-resistant ceramic tile floor is easy to maintain. However, its cold, hard surface offers no cushion while you stand on it and can be slippery when wet. To alleviate discomfort and ensure safety, add fluffy bath rugs.

Tips for cleaning tile: Scrub the floor with soap and water or a nonabrasive household cleaner. Don't wax. When the grout between the tiles becomes stained from contact with moisture, bleach it with grout bleach and a toothbrush. Seal the grout with a latex grout sealer after bleaching it.

Furniture Good storage is key to an orderly bathroom and makes the time you spend there more relaxing.

To make the hanging cupboard, *right*, sand an old bookcase and paint it white. Measure the height and width of the bookcase between the side rails where you plan to attach the door hinges. Cut two doors of plywood, each the height of the bookcase front and half its width less ⅛ inch on all sides. (The ⅛ inch is clearance so doors won't rub each other when opening and closing.) Cut a lath strip to match the height of the doors. Sand and paint the doors and lath. Rout pockets on the insides of the doors to accept the hinges. Affix the hinges to the doors and the side rails of the cabinet. Attach the strip of lath on the edge of one door to cover the slight gap between the doors. Lay the cabinet flat on its back, doors up. Center bamboo mats on each door and hot-glue them in place. To frame the bamboo insets, measure around the mats. Cut frames for the insets from molding; cut rabbets along the inside edges of the molding strips for a slight overlap on the bamboo mats. Paint the frames white. When dry, attach them to the doors around the mats (use a nail set to set in the nails; cover with wood filler). Touch up with paint and add door handles.

To make the small shelf for over the sink, *opposite*, follow the instructions for the hanging shelf on page 93. To install the shelf, invert it so the hanging rail is on the underside of the ledge rather than at the top.

A hanging cabinet, placed well off the floor, gives a visual lift to the room while leaving space below for a scale or shoes.

Substitution: sink backsplashes

If a glossy painted backsplash strikes you as insufficient, add three or four ceramic tiles to the wall above the sink. Use dark tiles to match the floor or plain, smooth white ones to match the sink. Dark tiles would call attention to themselves in a predominantly pale space such as this. White tiles would merely extend the white sink structure.

2

A ready-to-assemble storage tower, manufactured for use in closets, comes out into the light.

A metal towel ladder, attached to the wall, reaches for the ceiling, contributing strong vertical lines and convenient storage space.

A small sign on the door adds a
sense of fun to the bathroom entry.

WC

Mirrors are functional and
artistic additions to bathrooms.

3

Special touches, while
serving no practical
purpose, turn a bathroom
into a relaxing
spa-like space.

SáVON
de-
ME

accessories Because a bathroom is designated for grooming, mirrors and lights are essential to its function. When purchasing light bulbs for your bathroom, select those designed for vanity illumination; bulbs that are too yellow or too white will not accurately reflect how you look outside the bathroom. Several types of mirrors function well for grooming but also serve to reflect the light in the room, bouncing it around the space for more balanced lighting. A quality vanity mirror tops the list of mirrors for the bath. For maximum clarity and natural style, avoid frosted-glass mirrors or mirrors etched with motifs. For shaving or applying makeup, attach a magnifying mirror with an extendable arm to the bathroom wall near an electrical socket. If you dress in your bathroom, fasten a full-length mirror on the side of a storage tower, on the back of the door, or on a wall.

Door sign. Shop mail-order catalogs, the Internet, and specialty shops for small signs appropriate to bathrooms: "To ensure privacy, close the door," "the Loo," or "Le Bain," (The Bath). Attach the sign to the bathroom door with the small nails provided with the sign.

Stones. Naturally connected to water and bathing, stones make soothing additions to a bathroom. Smooth gray stones with white stripes evoke memories of Mediterranean beaches. Round pebbles draw you back to the depths of Lake Erie. Angular chunks put you in white-water streams or remind you of nights in a steamy Nordic sauna.

Weathered mirror. To make your own custom mirror, find a salvaged window with no more than one dividing bar (too many mullions fragment the mirror reflection). Remove the window glass. If the frame is painted, strip it of paint. Take the frame to a glazier to fit the glass openings with mirror panels. Hang the finished mirror so the bottom edge is no more than 40 inches from the floor. If the top of the mirror is tilted away from the wall, its bottom edge can be as much as 48 inches above the floor.

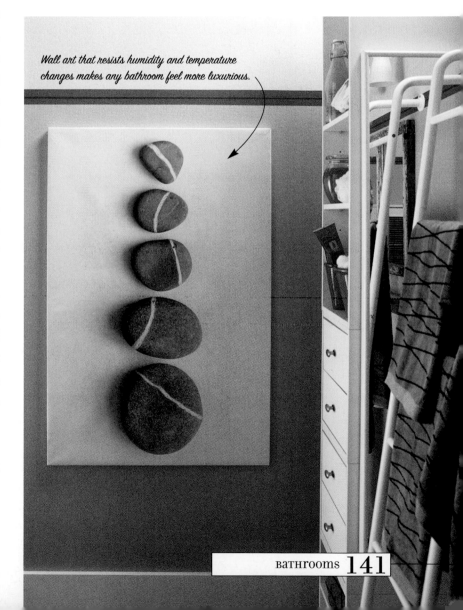

Wall art that resists humidity and temperature changes makes any bathroom feel more luxurious.

Take a romantic soak in the tub amid rustic furnishings and accessories with refined flourishes.

water music

1 BACKGROUND

WALL COLOR pastel pink

WINDOW COVERINGS sheer cotton panels

FLOOR COVERINGS terra-cotta tile; tapestry rug

FIXED LIGHTING overhead fixture

2 FURNITURE

FIXED red claw-foot tub; sink; toilet

FREESTANDING reddish-tone armoire; classic end table

WALL-HUNG red wire planter

3 accessories

MOOD LIGHTING romantic wall sconces; tubside lamp

PERSONAL COMFORTS fluffy white towels and bathrobe; books; bath salts; sponges; body washes; classical CDs

ROMANTIC TOUCHES crystal soap dish; candles; flowers

Paint the walls a gentle pink pastel. Choose the color from the palest pink-to-white palette. If your claw-foot tub is white, paint the outside of it with cherry red paint. Lay a tapestry rug in the center of the room and hang white curtains at the windows.

Arrange the armoire at the end of the tub or in a space where it serves best for accessible storage. Set a small, end table near the tub. Paint an antique planter red and hang it on the wall for towel storage. It will look like sculpture when white towels set off its woven wire sides.

Accessorize your space with classic, romantic pieces and personal comforts that beckon you to relax. Romantic style involves layers of texture, color, patina, and evocative details, such as flickering candlelight casting shadows on the wall or a sheer curtain that dances in the breeze. Hang flirty sconces, accented by silk shades and curled tendrils, above the armoire; add a sweet lamp to the tubside table. Stir up a bathtub potion: Mix 1 cup each of baking soda, Epsom salts, and citric acid (available at drugstores) in a large bowl. Gradually add to the mixture a drop each of various essential oils. Lavender relieves anxiety; rosemary and thyme revitalize. Stir ingredients thoroughly. Transfer ingredients from the bowl into a glass container, such as a jam jar. Seal it tightly; shake well. Draw a warm bath, adding 1 to 2 tablespoons of the mixture. Sink in and soak for at least 20 minutes.

—bath salt recipe by Kate Carter Frederick

Food for thought...

While you're in the tub, immerse your mind as well as your body. For romantic tomes, check out *Wuthering Heights*, a novel by Emily Bronte; it's a tale of complex, passionate love. *I Love You, Ronnie*, is a collection of Ronald Reagan's love letters to Nancy. *National Geographic Traveler* is a chance to take a honeymoon in your daydreams.

A red-painted claw-foot tub and antique planter set the tone and the scale for romancing this bath.

Terra-cotta tile is a natural for grounding a room and resisting watery treads from wet feet.

A tapestry rug is an unexpected luxury for guests.

Bold graphic letters energize a clean white space.

White ceramic tile wraps the room and creates an envelope of space open to any decorative style. With only a few accessories, it can become chic, casual, romantic, or classic.

Substitutions: shower curtains

To create your own custom shower curtain, begin with a plain, white cotton shower curtain from the home store. Iron on letters purchased from a crafts store or take the curtain to a T-shirt printing store to have the letters professionally adhered. Hang a plastic liner behind the curtain before use.

Hang dull shower curtains out to dry and replace them with draperies that send a custom-made message about your personal style.

THE WET LOOK

 1 B a c k g r o u n d

WOODWORK AND WALL TILE COLOR white

WINDOW COVERINGS white miniblinds

FLOOR COVERINGS white ceramic tile; blue throw rug

FIXED LIGHTING recessed lights; glass-block window light

 2 F u r n i t u r e

FIXED claw-foot tub; standard toilet and sink; medicine chest; linen closet

FREESTANDING wicker hampers

 3 a c c e s s o r i e s

FUN TOUCHES lettered shower curtain; blue curtain rings; tub toys

PERSONAL COMFORTS blue and white towels; rug; storage

Hire professionals to line the walls and floor of your bathroom with ceramic tile; you'll get a pure white box that's ready for water and the works. White is the symbol for clean and pure—dirt and grime can't hide in a white room. If you have a wood-frame window in the shower area, give it a glass-block update (1950s houses often come with wood-frame windows in tub/shower areas; these are ruined by water unless they're covered with plastic curtains of some sort). Replace the window with a vented glass-block window, scheduling the work so it will take place at the same time as the wall tile installation. A glass-block window, impervious to water, lights the space but provides privacy.

Reinstall the tub, toilet, and sink fixtures with the help of the contractor working on your bathroom project. Check the waterworks to see if everything is operating as you expect.

Personalize the space by putting words on a shower curtain. Ask a local banner or sign store to make the curtain for you, using the words and colors of your choice. Choose white exterior-banner material, which is made to be water- and mildew-resistant. At the same time, take towels that match or complement your curtain colors to a monogramming shop to have your word choice(s) embroidered onto the terry cloth. When the shower curtain is finished, hang it on a white rod with plastic rings that match the color theme. Then arrange the rest of the accessories in the bathroom— storage hampers, a tubside bench, or a glass caddy with nonslip rubber tips on its feet.

A blue and white scheme pleases those who honor tradition and long for touches of refinement in everyday things.

Classic Bath

 1 Background

WALL AND TRIM COLORS blue; white

WINDOW COVERINGS smocked eyelet curtains

FLOOR COVERINGS white-painted planking; rug

FIXED LIGHTING overhead fixtures

 2 Furniture

FIXED sink; tub/shower; toilet

FREESTANDING white armoire; white wicker chair

WALL-HUNG over-the-sink shelf

 3 accessories

CONVENIENCE magnifying mirror

PERSONAL COMFORTS artwork; hand towels

NATURAL TOUCH fresh flowers from the garden

Establish the color scheme for the room. Paint the walls blue and the woodwork white. If you have planked flooring, paint it white, using a floor-and-deck paint. Upgrade the overhead lighting, if desired—a crystal chandelier is an elegant and novel choice—and paint the ceiling white. For the windows, make soft cafe curtains from presmocked white eyelet (available at a fabric store). Or smock your own fabric by hand or machine; iron-on or sew-on smocking tape from the notions department makes the job quick and easy. Make the finished width of the smocked edge a few inches wider than the window width. Use coordinating fabric or satin ribbon to make hanging loops. Tack these straps to the smocked edge, leaving the loops long so they resemble spaghetti straps on a summer frock. Hang the curtain from a plain tension rod.

Add freestanding furniture. If you lack adequate storage for towels, tissue, cleaning supplies, purchase a freestanding armoire with shelves or bring in a storage unit with large drawers. Paint the storage unit white to blend with the woodwork. Attach a wall-hung shelf over the sink for additional storage of attractive items.

Accessorize the walls with classic artwork. Leave the over-the-sink shelf open for everyday grooming items. Store items that are used less often behind the closed doors of the white storage piece.

A slip of a window covering graces mullioned panes. Scallop-edged eyelet and smocking provide a summery look, regardless of the season.

An over-the-sink wall-hung shelf relieves the lack of surface space around the sink.

Like rolling skies filled with clouds, blue walls pair perfectly with white woodwork and accessories.

The old-time lines of exposed, antique plumbing bring sculpture, story, and fantasy to a simple bathing room.

Hold the stencil in place with painter's tape; apply acrylic paint in a pouncing motion with a stencil brush.

Stencil motifs pointing in multiple directions keep the rug design lively and natural.

Invite the outdoors in with natural fibers and from-the-forest forms and hues. With the addition of a stenciled pattern, a bamboo rug becomes a personalized work of art.

natural beauty

 1 BACKGROUND

WALL AND TRIM COLORS corn silk yellow; white

WINDOW COVERINGS bamboo blinds

FLOOR COVERINGS natural wood planking; bamboo rug

FIXED LIGHTING overhead milk-glass fixtures

 2 FURNITURE

FIXED tub; pedestal sink; toilet with pull-string flush;

corner cupboard

FREESTANDING yellow tubside table

 3 accessories

PERSONAL COMFORTS tubside soap dish; natural sponge;

fluffy white robes and towels

NATURAL TOUCHES green plants; nature artwork framed in

natural wood

Paint the walls a corn silk color in an eggshell finish. Paint the woodwork white in a high-gloss finish for easy clean-ups and wipe-downs. For a nonslip floor-covering, buy a 4×6-foot bamboo mat to stencil with leafy fronds. To decorate the mat, cut two stencils of the same design from acetate or cardboard (two stencils allow you to flip the pattern without waiting for paint to dry on a single stencil). Before painting, arrange paper frond cutouts on the mat in a pleasing pattern. Then replace the cutouts with a taped-on stencil and apply fern green acrylic paint with a stencil brush. When the printed images are dry, brush on varnish to protect them from bath splashes or dampness.

Arrange a small table beside the tub for easy access to bathing necessities or stock the table with pretty objects that add to the natural setting.

Accessorize with nature. Natural beauties, such as an easy-care orchid or framed pictures of butterflies, insects, and birds, bring the outdoors inside. To add to the leafy theme of the stenciled rug, gather leaves in the fall and press them between the pages of a telephone book to flatten and dry them out. Then mount them in ready-made mat-and-frame sets from an art or crafts supply store and hang them above the tub.

Furniture in the bathroom warms a cool, utilitarian space and weaves charm and function together.

eurostyle spa

1 BACKGROUND

WALL AND CEILING COLORS blue; white

WINDOW AND SHOWER COVERINGS gold fabric panels

FLOOR COVERINGS white ceramic tile; blue bath rug

FIXED LIGHTING overhead fixture; over-the-sink downlights

2 Furniture

FIXED pedestal corner sink; tub; toilet

FREESTANDING vanity table; wall-hung medicine chest

3 accessories

MOOD LIGHTING wall-hung candleholder

EUROPEAN TOUCHES antique letters; imported bath goods; soap dish; decorative mirrors with white frames; handheld showerhead; fresh flowers; oval wall-hung mirror

To design your own bathroom wainscot, pick up tile remnants and have a local bath and tile business put together the finished pieces for you. For the tub skirt, piece together the surface using parts of a salvaged door and corbels. After the tub skirt is assembled and fastened under the lip of the tub, seal the skirt with caulking. When the tile, floor, and tub skirt are complete, paint the ceiling white and add a floral border around the ceiling edges. Paint the tub skirt with white high-gloss waterproof marine paint for a seamless look. Then paint the walls with a semigloss blue. For the shower curtain, hang long gold panels attached to chrome rings that are supported by cable-cord window hardware fastened to the ceiling (see the small photograph, *opposite*).

Top a vanity table with bath tile remnants for a special piece of tubside furniture. Wearing eye protection, toss the tile in a canvas bag and hammer the bag to break the tile into small bits. Line the tabletop with tar paper. Set the tile on it and grout it. Then seal the tabletop with silicone tile sealant to withstand splashes and soap scum. Paint the table with the same high-gloss paint you used on the tub skirt. Hang a white-painted medicine chest over the vanity table.

Add personal touches to give the space the charm of a European bed-and-breakfast. For example, display large antique letters spelling "BATH" and fill glass bowls with luxury soaps. Add bottles of bath suds and perfumes to give yourself that getaway feeling you experienced on vacation.

Apply design opportunities to ceilings. A border adds beauty overhead.

A shower dressed with a formal drapery-style curtain adds cozy European charm.

A vanity table topped with bath tile remnants recalls the charm of European hotels.

A salvaged door and corbels form a charming tub skirt.

green
rooms

Everyone deserves to live in beauty. If one room of your home is designed as a gallery for Mother Nature's art, your appetite for natural beauty is sure to be satisfied. The first part of this chapter shows how a green thumb stirs a pot of ingredients to come up with a relaxing plant pavilion. Erasing the boundaries between indoors and out, all the green rooms in this chapter show you how to give your a home a generous helping of sunshine and natural beauty.

This green room recipe mixes together an earthy blend of colors and textures borrowed from the out-of-doors. Think of it as an indoor tent where you can sit among plants and other green things, safely sheltered from the wind and rain.

airy pavilion

1   BACKGROUND

WALL AND TRIM COLORS two soft, earthy greens

FLOOR COVERINGS faux stone tiling; sisal area rug

FIXED LIGHTING ceiling fixture

2   Furniture

SEATING sage green wicker chairs; upholstered bench

TABLES wood-and-iron coffee table; nesting tables; plant stand

STORAGE wooden folding shelf; bamboo tansu chest

3   accessories

MOOD LIGHTING glass candle lanterns; natural light

PERSONAL COMFORTS cushions; magazine racks

GREEN TOUCHES plants; green glass bottle and float collection; garden pots; birdcage; wall planter

Unadorned windows let maximum light flow into a room.

1

A pale, earthy backdrop awaits the arrival of natural greens from the garden.

Laminate flooring, styled in a stone design, brings the look of a terrace inside.

A sisal or straw area rug, purchased by the square, puts natural texture underfoot.

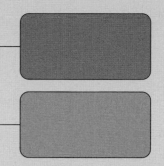

WALLS To select green room colors, zero in on the "dustier" tones (the colors that seem grayed-down when compared to the brightness of saturated colors) on the paint chip rack at your local paint store. Select from green tones that lean toward the yellow-greens rather than the blue-greens. Look for greens that represent burnished cornfields and mossy forests. Choose two greens next to each other on the paint strip, using the lighter one for walls, the darker one for woodwork.

BaCKGrouND If you like the clean-lined, modern look of the base and crown moldings in this room, remove existing moldings in your soon-to-be-green space. In a stripped-down interior, it's easy to decorate from the ground up.

For new moldings, cut 1×6 boards for base moldings and 1×2 boards for crown moldings. Miter 1×3 boards for door and window frames. Before installing them, paint them with the trim color—the darker green of the two greens you've selected for the room. Paint the walls pale green before installing the painted moldings.

To lay the "stone" flooring, have a professional installer measure and cut look-alike stone laminate to fit the space. A good installer—or a smart do-it-yourselfer—will avoid beginning at the corner of a room. The installer will also be wary of less-than-square corners in a room and have the right tools on hand to professionally cut the laminate.

Lay the area rug over the laminate flooring, placing the rug so that a 24-inch-wide border of faux stone surrounds it.

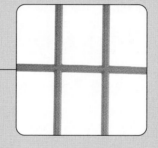

WINDOWS To prepare French doors for painting, use this professional painter's trick: Remove the doors and take them outside. Using a paint sprayer, cover the surfaces of the doors—even the glass—with paint. Then, with a single-edge razor in a utility dispenser, scrape the paint from the glass. The paint will slip off easily if you scrape it within an hour of spray-painting the doors.

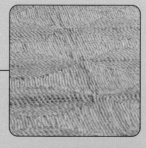

FLOOR COVERINGS Visit a flooring gallery in search of stone look-alikes. Use a project calculator to figure out how much square footage you'll need. For a sisal area rug, go to an import store that sells flooring by the square foot. The standard width is 9 feet, but you'll have a choice for the length.

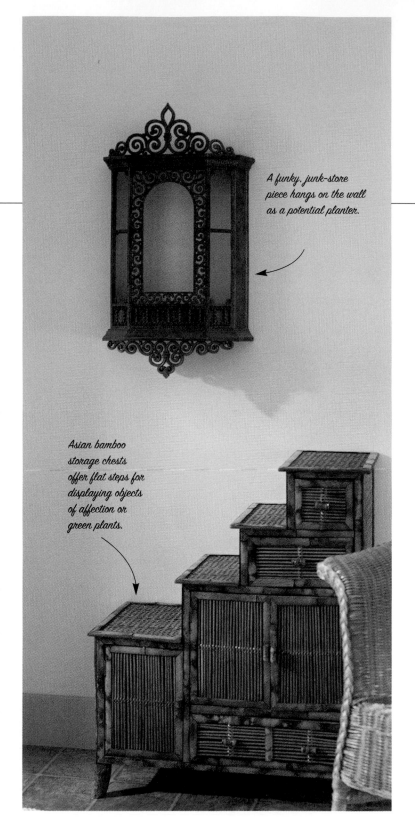

A funky, junk-store piece hangs on the wall as a potential planter.

Asian bamboo storage chests offer flat steps for displaying objects of affection or green plants.

FURNITURE that blurs the boundaries between indoors and out is essential in the making of a green room. Casual furniture markets, import shops, and seasonal stores offer inventories of wicker, iron, bamboo, and wood furniture pieces that translate well into the language of indoor-outdoor spaces.

To find inexpensive green room furniture, cruise the aisles of discount stores, which are well-stocked with casual furniture in early spring. You'll find storage pieces such as the bamboo tansu chest, *right*. You'll also find small chests with drawers, end tables, plant stands, and stools. Look for small iron cafe-style table-and-chairs sets and remember that outdoor furniture often functions quite well inside. Another idea: Search antiques malls and shops for a table and chairs from an old-fashioned ice-cream parlor. In general, anchor the room with a large, serviceable coffee table and surround it with comfortable, casual seating. Then add storage pieces for plants, such as shelves, benches, and floor stands that roll around on wheels.

2

Like supporting players, three matching wicker chairs face the iron bench, adding to its star quality in the room.

A tall vertical shelf unit balances the low horizontal lines of the seating pieces and provides ample storage for personal collections of green things.

A low seating piece plays the role of garden bench and becomes the star attraction.

Sidekick chairside tables offer arm's-length convenience and display for pretty objects.

Located centrally in the room, a square coffee table anchors the gathering spot and seating pieces.

Natural muslin pillows with green chenille swirls are a fitting choice for green room cushions.

Lanterns and candles bring on the romance of evenings at a beach, a park, a campground, or a cabin in the woods.

3

A vibrant collection of green glass bowls, vases, and floats glitters in the sunlight, adding beauty to an airy green pavilion.

accessories

A green room comes to life with the addition of plants. To keep them in good company, add cushions, beautiful pots, and the gleam of green glass.

Cushions. Soften the seating pieces and add decoration to the room with ready-made pillows—or make them yourself. To make the swirl pillows, *opposite,* buy muslin, avocado green cotton, green thread, yellow-green chenille cording, and pillow stuffing. Using a random pattern over the yardage, decorate one yard with chenille swirls. Pick a starting point and begin a zigzag stitch (thread your sewing machine in green) to fasten down one end of the chenille cord. Using the sewing-machine foot as the measure for the space between the cord lines, continue fastening the cord as you turn the fabric in a circle. Moving outward as you go, circle around ten times to complete the swirl. Repeat the swirls randomly over the muslin. When the fabric is decorated, cut it into 18-inch squares for pillow fronts. For pillow backs, cut matching squares from green cotton. Make knife-edge pillows by matching fronts and backs, right sides facing, and sewing them together ¾ inch from the raw edges. Leave 5-inch openings on one side of each pillow for turning. Turn right side out, stuff, and hand-stitch the pillows closed.

Plants and pots. To begin collecting green pottery, haunt garden stores, import stores, discount stores, and seasonal stores for ceramic and terra-cotta pots. These stores also sell plants so purchase a few and pot them. Avoid cheap plastic greenery, which detracts from the natural scheme.

Green glass. Every room needs glitter and gleam. In many rooms, shiny metals provide the glamour. Garden rooms, where matte black wrought iron often is king, call for an entirely different material: glass. Gathering glass for your green room is a fun project: Walk store aisles, scanning for green glass, and you'll come up with an amazing variety. Glass orbs (fishing floats), blown-glass balls, bowls, plates, cups, vases, bottles, and lanterns can be had for a song.

Green rooms need green plants. A good collection of greenery mixes textures and shapes.

One of the pleasures of a second-floor apartment is a small balcony off the living room or bedroom. Here, lush potted plants and old furniture combine to create a serene Sunday-morning getaway.

comfort zone

 1 BACKGROUND

WALLS wooden fencing; iron railing; trees

FLOOR COVERING cedar planking

FIXED LIGHTING natural light

 2 Furniture

TABLE tile-top table with wrought-iron base

SEATING green park bench

STORAGE plant display rack

 3 accessories

MOOD LIGHTING candles; lanterns; moonlight

GREEN THINGS plants in terra-cotta pots; plantings

borrowed from the landscape

Relax and recharge your spirit—that's the house rule for Sunday mornings. If you're renting an apartment, chances are there is little you can do to change the backdrop of your balcony space. It probably comes with a safety railing and privacy walls, so the first decorating ingredient is already in the mix. Keep your background elements in mind as you develop the space. For example, the wrought-iron railing, weathered cedar walls, and wood floor of this space offer decorating cues. A wrought-iron table base and weathered wood planter echo the natural materials of the backdrop.

Green room furniture that is precious or fragile spells discomfort. When picking furnishings for an outdoor balcony, ask yourself these questions: Is it comfortable? Does it feel good to sit on, walk over, and touch? Is it visually pleasing? Does it fit naturally, or does it look self-conscious? Is it weather-worthy, or does it need special maintenance? New outdoor furniture is nice but not necessary. Antique pieces (as long as they don't scream "hands off") create a sense of settled relaxation; furniture that looks a little worn is naturally comfortable.

Choose weather-worthy accessories and easily transported items that can be brought out for the day. Plants are an obvious choice for softening the hard edges of railings and tabletops. A collection of watering cans is interesting to look at and useful as well. A good rule for the green thumb: Plant your posies in only one style of pot. A gang of mismatched pots adds up to junky junk, while a collection of one kind has unity, balance, and focal-point power.

A horizontal bank of pots in a planter softens the vertical planks of a privacy wall.

Substitutions: Sunday getaways

So you don't have a balcony—think of other getaways, such as a corner in a master bedroom or an alcove off the kitchen. Consider a spot on a patio or porch when weather allows; use an attic, a bay window, or a stair landing in inclement weather. Keep your retreat away from household traffic patterns and define it with a threshold, such as a high-back sofa or a small area rug. If your space is limited, create a room within a room by adding curtains to a four-poster bed. Or turn an ordinary love seat into a haven with a stack of plush pillows.

The curves of a wrought-iron table base play in tune with the wrought-iron balcony railing, creating harmony and a lyrical quality for this getaway.

A ladder-like etagere stacks plants at different levels, exposing each one to maximum sunlight.

Light-welcoming windows, kept free of heavy fabric, allow the plants plenty of sun.

Framed botanical prints enhance the natural theme of the room.

The occasional leafy texture and burst of flower color balance the look of a room and bring it to life. Here's how to live comfortably with plants.

POTTING MIX

1 Background

WALL AND TRIM COLORS soft yellow, white

WINDOW COVERINGS sheer white panels on metal rods

FLOOR COVERINGS wood floor; area carpet

FIXED LIGHTING ceiling fixture; natural light

2 Furniture

SEATING slipcovered sofa; wicker side chair

TABLES bamboo nesting tables; antique sideboard

PLANT DISPLAY wrought-iron planters; étagère

3 accessories

PERSONAL COMFORTS cushions

GREEN TOUCHES plants; botanical prints; plant cloches; terra-cotta pots; hanging basket

Paint the walls pale yellow and trim them with white woodwork for a neutral backdrop that shows green plants at their natural best. Hang light fabric at the windows to allow for a maximum flow of natural light. Establish the seating area with an area rug.

Arrange furniture to create an island of comfort for yourself toward the center of the room. This leaves space for plants near windows, where they can get the benefit of sunlight. Choose furnishings with a natural bent that will complement plants: greens and tans are good color choices; wood, wicker, and natural fabrics make perfect green room construction materials.

Potted plants make naturally beautiful accessories. When choosing the right plant for the room, think about the kind of light the room receives. Also consider size, color, and texture while selecting plants. Pick those that are proportionally matched to the room dimensions as well as to each other. Play with texture—for example, contrast the hard edges of a cactus with the soft spill of ferns. Vary the array of leaf shapes, colors, and fullness. Master display choices—terra-cotta clay pots are simple and serviceable, but consider a selection of terrariums and cloches that provide greenhouse conditions in which plants thrive. Round out these glass enclosures with a limited selection of ceramic pots or woven baskets, and hangers for floor-to-ceiling options of plant arranging. Position plants at varying heights around the room for a balanced effect and protect furniture surfaces from leaks by placing trays or nonporous plates under pots.

A front porch without a swing is like a summer without sun. Here's how to hang a glider that will stand up to summer rains all season long.

room to swing

1   B a c k g r o u n d

WALL COLORS white

FLOOR COVERINGS stone aggregate or porch planking

FIXED LIGHTING natural light

2   F u r n i t u r e

SEATING old-fashioned porch swing; porch chairs

TABLES folding trays

3   a c c e s s o r i e s

PERSONAL CONVENIENCES cushions; tray service

GREEN THINGS potted plants; plants borrowed from landscape beyond

VINTAGE TOUCH antique framed glass

Paint the porch interior white—if white works with the exterior colors of your house. White is the perfect color for framing green views beyond the porch. Neighboring trees, shrubs, and flowers are an ever-present, maintenance-free panorama of lush vegetation to enjoy at a distance.

Hang the swing after painting it with a distressed antique white finish (sand the wood to make uneven surfaces). Instead of hanging the swing from eyebolts in the porch ceiling, add a pair of high-tension springs between the bolts and the chain. The springs give a little bounce and make the gliding action smooth and easy. Pull up porch chairs in a group facing the swing to create a green room. Add folding trays for neighbors and friends that come by for a swing.

Soften the porch swing and chairs with a collection of toss pillows, keeping their colors and patterns in quiet, natural tones and shapes. Inside the house, keep a stash of porch serving pieces—iced tea pitchers, glasses, and napkins are easy to retrieve from the kitchen at a moment's notice. For an added artistic touch and a conversation piece, hang a framed window of etched glass from a porch rafter behind the swing.

A panel of etched glass pretends to be a window.

Borrowed scenery is viewed from the open windows of a porch.

Dress an old-fashioned porch in summertime style.

Despite its unconventional shape, the room harmonizes with the original house because roofing and siding materials are the same.

A shelf above three windows makes room for a collection of white ceramics.

Casement windows scoop up sunshine and scenery without overwhelming the space. The simulated divided-light units feature a muntin grid that matches the other windows of the house.

Food for thought...

When adding a green room onto an existing home, build it as part of the house, rather than a screened-in porch. This octagonal design, reminiscent of a gazebo, doesn't feel like an outdoor structure that was simply fitted with windows and filled with furniture. An addition of the house, the birch ceiling—finished with a golden oak stain to accentuate the grain—matches oak woodwork throughout the rest of the home. Likewise, the cream-color ceramic tile and walls complement the neutral finishes in nearby rooms.

Whether you build a new sunroom or redecorate one that already exists, here's a decorating scheme that creates a warm and cozy atmosphere.

sun space

 1 BaCKGround

WALL, CEILING AND TRIM COLORS cream; white; golden oak wood stain over birch ceiling and shelving

WINDOW COVERINGS natural-tone Roman shades

FLOOR COVERING cream-color ceramic tile

 2 Furniture

SEATING two upholstered armchairs, wicker love seat and matching chair; wicker dining chairs

TABLES glass-top cafe table; side tables; wood bench

 3 accessories

LIGHTING ceiling-hung fan/lights; ceramic-base lamps

PERSONAL COMFORTS cushions; throw; soft ottoman

GREEN TOUCHES ceramic pots; creamware collection; green plants; plant stands

Apply wood stain. Golden oak stain on a wood ceiling brings out the natural grain of the timber. Paint walls a butter-cream color, trim the window frames in bright white, and stain the shelving over the windows the same tone as the ceiling. Hang toast-color Roman shades (these are professionally fabricated from a muted stripe fabric) and add a ceiling fan with lights at the center of the room.

Furnish generously. Fill a spacious sunroom with generously proportioned, casual pieces that create a warm and welcoming mood and feel comfortable all year round. Think natural and neutral; when choosing wood pieces, choose light ones rather than dark ones. The centerpiece for this room is a wicker settee placed directly opposite the entrance to the room. Because the shape of the room is octagonal, it suggests a loose, relaxed circle of seating pieces around the coffee table in front of the settee. Side tables, inserted between chairs, offer chairside conveniences, such as coffee cups, water glasses, and reading material. Space allows for a cafe-style table and chairs that make the perfect spot for sunny breakfasts.

Personal touches. Seating pieces with cushions and tabletops with armchair conveniences, such as white ginger-jar lamps for reading, bowls for fruit, and potted plants for accents, invite relaxation. Arrange a display of appealing white creamware pitchers, bowls, and platters, or organize another collection that reflects your personal interests, on an overhead shelf.

This modern take on traditional style combines elements fitting an older home: cottage colors, breezy fabrics, and wood pieces with a country feel.

cottage garden

 BACKGROUND

WALL AND TRIM COLORS pale green; white

WINDOW COVERINGS exterior English ivy

FLOOR COVERINGS terra-cotta tile; hooked area rug

FIXED LIGHTING skylight

 Furniture

SEATING natural wicker love seat and side chair; white upholstered desk chair

TABLES wood desk; antique tea cart; antique end tables

 accessories

PERSONAL COMFORTS plaid and floral fringed cushions; books; desk and table lamps; chenille throw

GREEN TOUCHES plants; flowers in glass vases

Paint walls pale green and wood trim white. An eggshell finish for wall paint is best; cover woodwork with satin or gloss finish for durability. Over a terra-cotta tile floor, lay an antique floral hooked rug. Note the placement in the room shown here. The rug is placed on an angle across the terra-cotta tile to ready the room for a seating arrangement set on the diagonal. Leave windows uncovered if a screen of greenery, such as English ivy, is planted along the exterior of the house. **Choose furniture** pieces for their personal value rather than for their pedigrees or price tags. To supplement family heirlooms, shop auctions, garage sales, and antiques stores to buy things you love. Anchor the back wall of the space with a large wood table to use as a generous writing desk. For a desk chair, slide in a comfortable upholstered slipper chair. Arrange wicker seating pieces at an angle in the room and roll in a tea cart to serve as a coffee table and bookshelf. Add end tables near seating pieces to hold lamps, cups, books, and dishes.

Find floral cushions with colors and designs that complement the focal-point area rug. Add a plaid pillow or two for contrast. Toss the cushions in a balanced arrangement and fill out the rest of the room with the softening touches of green plants and flowers. If space allows, place a tall metal planter behind the wicker sofa as a garden screen.

Pale green walls emphasize the white-painted traditional window framing.

Skylights open the room to the sunshine and the out-of-doors.

English ivy outside the house doubles as window coverings for the room.

Textural wicker furniture, floral prints, and terra-cotta tile evoke the mood of a cottage garden.

Substitution: personal objects

Substitute modern furnishings for antiques for a hip cottage garden. For example, replace brown wicker seating pieces with white or pale green wicker. Try a white-wood writing desk with a chair slipcovered in lime-green and white awning stripes. Replace the traditional rug with a bamboo area rug. For a coffee table in front of a green or white wicker love seat, find a glass-top table with a white-wood frame.

TOOLS AND MATERIALS

Like any recipe—cake, casserole, or appetizer—a decorating project calls for basic tools and materials. Putting a new face on an old room is more fun when you have the basics on hand and can move ahead whenever the urge to decorate comes on. In this chapter you'll find a directory of decorating staples—some familiar and already present in your decorating pantry, others to acquire for future projects.

decorator's pantry

TOOLS

WHAT TO LOOK FOR	WHAT IT IS	HOW TO USE IT
	CARPENTER'S PENCIL A sturdy marking tool with a flat body, this pencil contains a thick stem of lead that doesn't break. It makes a definite, easily seen mark on lumber.	Sharpen it with a pocketknife when necessary; mark lumber, such as picture-framing material, wainscot, beaded board, or moldings, before cutting with a saw.
	DRILL/DRIVER/SAW SET A triple-duty power tool, the drill/driver/saw drills holes, drives screws, and cuts small lumber pieces. Cordless models let you move freely about the room as you work.	This tool has many uses. For example, when hanging window hardware, predrill screw holes using the drill bits that come with the set. Then change to the screwdriver attachment to drive in the screws.
	HAMMER This hand tool—consisting of a handle with a perpendicularly attached head of heavy, rigid material—is used to drive nails and shape metal.	Pound picture-hanging hardware into walls to hang framed artwork and mirrors or remove unwanted nails with the claw. Also use the hammer to secure furniture joints.
	COMMON HARDWARE Cup hooks, screw eyes, open screw eyes, 1- and 2-inch nails, and screws with anchors are the hardware basics most often used in decorating.	Hang and/or display objects with open screw eyes and cup hooks. Secure wires or cords with screw eyes. Use anchored screws to hold objects securely on walls that don't have studs.
	LEVEL A device for determining whether a surface is perfectly horizontal, this tool holds a liquid-filled tube containing an air bubble that moves to a center window when the device is on a level plane.	Before painting rectangular or stripe designs on a wall, use the level as a vertical or horizontal guide for drawing perfect lines. Apply painter's tape along the lines to mask off the adjacent areas.
	METAL MEASURE A rigid measuring tool, this item is handy for determining small lengths on windows, walls, and floors.	Moving beyond measurements, use the straight edges of the metal to help you draw lines on fabric, wood, walls, or paper.
	POCKET LEVEL A miniature version of the standard level, this tiny tool hangs on a key chain or tool ring for convenience.	Use in tight places where a standard level doesn't fit. Check moldings and wall art to see if they're hanging straight.
	POCKETKNIFE This small set of tools is a convenient, portable item containing two cutting blades and a small scissors.	Keep it in a fanny pack or small decorating kit that you can find in a hurry when you need to cut threads or candlewicks, or open a box.
	MINI-MEASURING TAPE A tiny version of a carpenter's tape measure, this 3-yard-long measure fits neatly in a purse or pocket.	Take this tool shopping and measure the sizes of decorative objects to see if they'll fit in your available space. (Remember to take home measurements with you.)
	MINIATURE SCREWDRIVERS Like the full-size set, this pair consists of a slotted and a phillips screwdriver.	Use them for tiny screws. For example, tighten loosened screws on a makeup mirror or readjust your sewing machine. Keep them with your other miniature tools.
	SMALL WRENCH A bar of metal with an adjustable jaw, this tool catches, grips, turns, and twists the head of a bolt, nut, or pipe.	Keep it with your miniature tool kit and use it for the tiniest nuts and bolts on home furnishings, such as those on an adjustable mirror or lamp.
	NEEDLE-NOSE PLIERS As its name implies, these pliers have a long, narrow nose for pinching and twisting. Rubber-grip handles ensure a secure hold on the tool.	Use it for twisting florist wire (while assembling a bouquet), picture wire (when fastening it to a frame), or electrical wire (when wiring a lamp or ceiling fixture).

WHAT TO LOOK FOR	WHAT IT IS	HOW TO USE IT
	NO. 2 LEAD PENCIL A typical writing tool, the pencil can be sharpened to a narrow point in readiness for your next wall painting project.	In conjunction with a level or straightedge, draw light pencil lines on a wall to prepare for painting stripes or for hanging a towel bar, a curtain rod, a picture rail, or a plywood panel.
	PICTURE-HANGING HARDWARE Small hooks and nails that fit through the guides in the hooks are made especially for hanging pictures. Small hooks hold up to 20 pounds; large ones, as much as 50 pounds.	Hold the hanger against the wall. Insert the nail into the guide and tap gently into the wall using light hammer strokes. The needle-point nails will penetrate wall plaster easily. Reuse the hangers.
	PICTURE-HANGING WIRE Sometimes called mirror cord, this No. 6 braided, galvanized metal wire is made specifically for hanging pictures and mirrors on the wall.	Measure the length across the picture and add 8-12 inches; cut with a wire cutter. Thread ends through screw eyes on either side of the picture and loop them back onto the wire. Twist for a few turns, change direction, and twist until secure.
	SLIP-JOINT PLIERS These small pincers with long jaws bend wire and hold small objects in a tight grip. Nonslip cushion grips are for comfort only (they don't protect against electric shock).	Tighten bolts, remove stripped screws, twist two wires together, clamp two items together, grasp and pull out wires, and open containers with small tops. Slip the joint to a wider position to grasp larger items.
	POWER STAPLER Like the office stapler that fastens layers of paper together, this more powerful gadget makes light work of fastening together heavier materials.	Staple fabric to a cornice on a window treatment. Attach upholstery to a chair or a wall. Stretch a canvas or decorative fabric around a wood frame.
	SAFETY GLASSES These spectacles with transparent side flaps or fenders protect eyes from flying staples, wood dust, or other decorating debris.	Wear them while working on decorating processes that cause flying debris. For more-dangerous decorating or remodeling, such as sandblasting, wear goggles that fit snugly around the head.
	SCREWDRIVER SET Used for driving in or withdrawing screws, a screwdriver set is made up of two types: the slotted or flat-ended driver that fits into screw heads with one slot, and the screwdriver with a pointed and crossed end (known as the phillips screwdriver) that fits screws with crossed heads.	Match the screwdriver to the head of the screw you wish to turn, push weight against the point, and turn until the screw is embedded in the material. Use a screwdriver to assemble flat-pack furniture or to remove and return switchplates while painting walls. In a pinch, use it to open paint cans.
	PUTTY KNIFE This hand tool with a flat blade and a lightweight handle comes in a variety of sizes for various purposes. Buy the one that fits your needs.	Use this thin blade to "putty" windows (secure panes of glass), fill holes in woodwork, put a finishing coat on plaster, or apply a rough coat of drywall compound on a wall for a stucco look.
	STUD FINDER A battery-operated tool that finds wood studs inside the wall, this item is handy for hanging pictures, shelves, and cabinets on the walls.	Slowly slide the unit horizontally across the wall, right or left. Red light and/or "beep" indicates edge of stud. Screw wall-hung items into stud locations.
	CARPENTER'S TAPE MEASURE A plastic or metal palm-size case with a pullout ruler, this tool automatically pulls its ruler back into the case at the touch of a button.	Measure the lengths of walls, floors, windows, curtains, wallcovering borders, and rugs. The information gained from measuring moves your decorating projects forward to the finish.

DECORATING FILES/CUTTING TOOLS

WHAT TO LOOK FOR	WHAT IT IS	HOW TO USE IT
	DECORATING BOOKS A library of books filled with rooms that inspire decorating dreams is something every homeowner needs.	Visit bookstores and libraries to look at photos of design and decor in homes of every style. Purchase books that reflect your sensibilities; buy others because they will guide you through the steps of decorating projects you would like to do.
	DECORATING SAMPLES Paint chips, fabric swatches, and tile or wood samples inspire and inform decorating plans.	Collect samples. Visit a paint store, home center, or fabric store to gather free bits of color and texture that will be the seeds for your next project. Bring them out when it's time to make decorating decisions.
	DECORATING DIARY Like a journal or personal diary, a collection of tear sheets from magazines creates a composite picture of you and your desires. From desire comes action. If you haven't made the first step toward creating a picture of your decorating self, start your decorating diary today.	Clip and save. Collect magazine pictures of rooms that inspire you. Collect print images that evoke particular moods for you. Tuck them into a book, a folder, or a file next to your magazine tear sheet collection. Map out a decorating plan.

CUTTING TOOLS

	CRAFTS KNIFE A narrow, sharp-pointed razor blade is attached to the end of a penlike handle for cutting control. Turn the holder to a releasing position to change the blade.	At a desk or table, use the crafts knife to cut mats for pictures. Also use it for creating paper artwork or cutting fine edges along a wallcovering border.
	SCISSORS A general-purpose shears is great for cutting light cardboard, tape, string, paper, and office materials. Plastic-covered handles offer a comfortable fit. For cutting fabric, buy a special fabric-cutting shears.	Use the general-purpose shears to cut wallcovering, crafts materials, and collages for decorating plans. Cut curtain, tablecloth, and bed-linen sewing projects with a fabric shears.
	GARDEN SHEARS Scissors for cutting flower stems come with notched blades to provide extra leverage when cutting woody material. Some shears can be taken apart for easy cleaning by hand or in the dishwasher.	Cut flower stems and small branches to bring inside for decorating purposes. Use the shears again to fine-tune the lengths of the stems for an arrangement in a vase.
	HEAVY-DUTY SNIPS This tool will cut almost anything—carpet, cloth, leather, linoleum, tinplate, branches. Blade serrations provide a firm grip on the material for effortless cutting.	Use the snips while upholstering dining room chairs, trimming do-it-yourself vinyl tile, or laying carpet. Keep blades clean and free of debris. Lightly oil the blades and pivot after each use.

cutting tools/glues and adhesives

WHAT TO LOOK FOR	WHAT IT IS	HOW TO USE IT
	RAZOR Also known as a window scraper, this single-edge razor blade resides in a small plastic holder. The plastic handle snaps open for changing blades or for storing the razor in a safe, reversed position.	After painting window trim and mullions on doors, use this razor to scrape away paint from the glass. It's also useful for cleaning sticky labels and candle wax from hard, smooth surfaces such as mirror or glass.
	UTILITY KNIFE A razor knife blade set at an angle for cutting cardboard, this sturdy tool is also known as a box cutter.	When mail-order furnishings arrive, cut open the boxes. A utility knife is also useful for cutting through plastic, rubber, and other heavy materials.
	WIRE CUTTER A clipper-like tool, this small hand device is made for cutting wire. Rubber-grip handles ensure a secure hold on the tool.	In decorating, it's used primarily for cutting mirror- and picture-hanging wire. Other uses include cutting electrical wire while assembling a lamp, or florist wire while designing a flower arrangement.

Glues and Adhesives

	GLUE PEN Liquid mucilage flows from a capsule in a controlled manner.	Fasten together lightweight materials such as paper, cardboard, photographs in an album, or a collage in a decorating diary.
	GLUE STICK A solid form of glue, this general-purpose adhesive is safe and easy to use.	Assemble paper projects, such as picture albums or custom-cut lampshades. Children can safely use a glue stick for school projects.
	HOT-GLUE GUN A favorite of hobbyists, this dispenser of hot, transparent adhesive can be dangerous because of its heat. Handle it carefully to avoid burning yourself.	Heat the glue gun before beginning a project, such as a decorative wreath or a shell border around a mirror. Follow manufacturer's instructions for handling the tool and replacing the glue. For safety, keep the gun upright on its stand between applications.
	SPRAY ADHESIVE This handy product dispenses glue in spray form. The advantage is a finer application than can be achieved with a glue gun, pen, or stick.	Follow manufacturer's instructions for applying. Fasten together layers of paper, light sheets of wood, cardboard, or other porous material.
	TACKY WAX As the name implies, this adhesive is a waxlike material that is tacky, not sticky. It performs somewhat like glue but can be easily removed without a trace.	Use tacky wax to hold small items in place on a display shelf. Tack lightweight items on walls or smooth surfaces for temporary display.
	WOOD GLUE Made especially for permanently fastening one piece of wood to another, this glue is recognizable by its yellowish tint.	Repair wood furniture with wood glue or assemble new pieces with it. Keep the cap tightly closed during storage or the glue will dry out.

surface repair/painting supplies

WHAT TO LOOK FOR	WHAT IT IS	HOW TO USE IT
	FABRIC PROTECTOR A spray application, this mist for fabric repels water and spills without changing the look or feel of the fabric. It beads up liquids and greasy spills before they turn into stains, protecting upholstered furniture, slipcovers, and quilts.	In a well-ventilated area, spray with a sweeping motion about 6 inches from the fabric with a speed that evenly wets the fabric. Allow fabric to dry before using (up to six hours). Test repellency with a few drops of water. If water soaks in, re-spray.
	SANDING PADS These resilient foam blocks have sanded surfaces of different grades on either side. They're more comfortable to hold than plain sandpaper and they're perfect for round or highly contoured surfaces. Buy pads designed for specific purposes—paint stripping, sanding bare surfaces, or sanding between coats.	Be done with clumsy homemade sanding blocks. Enjoy the cushioned comfort of a sanding pad while sanding wood, paint, metal, plastic, or drywall. Use sanding sponges either wet or dry; rinse and reuse.
	PATCHING STICK A small, convenient package complete with all the tools you need, this product handles small repair jobs that require patching plaster.	Fill gouges and scratches on walls by dispensing the compound and smoothing it with the blade attached to the cover.
	TUNG OIL This product is a quick, natural oil wood finish that's easy to apply. It brings out the natural grain of the wood, giving it a remarkably durable luster without the fuss of wood stains.	Apply tung oil with cheesecloth, wiping with the grain of the wood, not across it. After several months, the oil will dry and the wood will need another application.
	WOOD-SCRATCH ERASER This pencil-like container of wood filler heals small wounds and scratches on wood furniture.	Draw the "lead" of the pencil over the scratch, filling it in. Smooth the excess material away with your finger. Touch up the surface with stain.
	WOOD-FINISH MARKER Like a permanent marking pen for laundry, this wide-tipped felt pen dispenses wood stain.	Touch up scratches in wood furniture with this ready-to-go marker in a matching wood tone.

Painting supplies

	ARTIST'S BRUSHES Use a set of small brushes of various widths for either water- or oil-base paints. Check the labels to purchase the type that matches the paint you plan to use. Buy several—some tapered, others with blunt-cut ends.	Paint pictures, refine the edges of a painted wall finish, fill patches where masking tape pulled up paint, or add details to a stenciled design. Always clean the brushes at the end of each painting period and store in an upright position to prevent damage to the hairs.
	PAINTBRUSHES For painting with latex and water-base paints, nylon and polyester brushes hold their shape and resilience best. For oil-base paints, a natural bristle or a synthetic filament brush works the best. A bristle brush has better flow qualities and brushing characteristics. It also requires less dipping into the paint can.	With a new brush, work the brush back and forth across your fingers to remove any loose bristles. Always apply the paint in the direction of the wood grain. When applying paint, the best finish is obtained with the tips of the brush, not the sides. Always use a stir stick rather than a brush to stir paint. Clean brushes after each use.
	DROP CLOTH A protective cover of plastic or fabric, this sheet keeps furniture, appliances, and carpet safe from paint and debris while you redecorate walls or ceilings.	Unfold the fabric or pleated plastic and spread it over the surfaces that need protection.

WHAT TO LOOK FOR	WHAT IT IS	HOW TO USE IT
	PAINT ROLLER A paint applicator with an extendable handle, this roller extends to 24 inches and reaches up to 34 inches, eliminating the need to stand on a stepladder while painting ceilings.	Extend the handle, following the manufacturer's instructions. Dip the roller into a paint tray and roll paint on smooth or semismooth surfaces. While intended primarily for painting ceilings, the extendable roller is also useful on walls of varying heights.
	FOAM BRUSH Most paint applicators are made with long hairs or bristles. This applicator—a block of pliable foam at the end of a stick—is another good option for latex paint. It's easier to clean than a brush.	Dip the foam end of the brush into paint and spread the paint over a smooth or semismooth surface. Use the same motion as you would with a bristle brush. Clean with water.
	MINI-ROLLER/TRAY SET Paint manufacturers offer tiny paint sets—applicators with foam rollers and plastic containers that hold only small amounts of paint.	Ideal for small areas, mini-rollers can be used for all paints—latex, acrylic, alkyd—on smooth and semismooth surfaces.
	PAINTER'S TAPE Resembling masking tape, this roll of blue material is less sticky and leaves no sticky residue. Another form comes in a roll of adhesive-coated crafts paper that's easy to apply along straight edges of a painted wall treatment, such as a striped design.	Fasten it over walls, baseboards, windows, and trim to protect these areas from the paint you apply to adjacent surfaces. Clean all the surfaces before applying tape. On delicate surfaces, test in an inconspicuous area before applying. When paint is dry to the touch, carefully remove the tape.
	6-INCH PAINT ROLLER/TRAY SET Styled like the standard roller, this shorter version is handy for small areas. It's lightweight and easy to clean. The coordinating plastic tray holds an appropriate amount of paint.	Pour paint into the deep end of the tray. Dip the roller into the paint and press the roller on the ramp to spread the paint evenly over the roller. Repeat to load the roller with the desired amount of paint before applying it to a piece of furniture, a cabinet, or a color block on a wall.
	NATURAL SPONGE This sponge, harvested from the sea, has large pores that absorb and release liquid. When wet, it is pliable and extremely resilient.	Use a natural sea sponge for painted finishes on walls. Dampen the sponge with water to make it pliable, dab up the desired amount of paint, and press the color onto the wall in a gentle pouncing motion to create a "sponged" effect. Or use the sponge to apply color through the openings of a large stencil.
	STENCIL BRUSH A hand tool made especially for stenciling, this brush features bluntly cut bristles for flat application of paint through stencils.	In a pouncing motion, fill the brush bristles with the desired amount of stencil paint. Apply color through the openings of the stencil with the same pouncing movement.
	PAINT STIR STICKS Made especially for stirring paint, these inexpensive panels of wood are offered free with the purchase of a can of paint.	Open the paint can and insert the stick into the paint. Stir in a circular motion until the paint is uniform in color. Stir carefully to blend in the contents at the bottom of the can. This is especially important if the paint has been stored for a long time.

wallcovering/flower arranging supplies

WHAT TO LOOK FOR	WHAT IT IS	HOW TO USE IT
	WALLCOVERING CUTTING TOOLS A triangular trim guide with a snap-off utility knife has retractable blades and a built-in knife holder. The angled shape of the cutter allows for cutting into corners.	Remove the end cap/blade breaker and extend the blade to expose one blade only. Hold scored side of blade away from your body. Insert the knife into the trim guide holder and pull the blade across the wallcovering where you want the cut.
	PAPER-HANGING TOOL SET This common kit includes a large water pan, a smoothing blade, a sponge, roller, and cutting blade. You'll find it in the paint section at a home center or discount store.	Fill the pan half full with water. Draw a precut length of wallcovering through the water to wet it. "Book" the wallcovering for a few minutes; then attach to the wall. Smooth out any air bubbles under the wallcovering with the smoothing blade. Roll edges with the roller, wipe away excess water with the sponge, and trim corners with the cutting blade.
	WALLCOVERING SEAM REPAIR An adhesive made especially for wallcovering, this tube of white glue has a pointed tip for easy application.	Squeeze the tube to apply adhesive along edges that have loosened. Smooth with your fingertips until the wallcovering is fastened on the wall; wipe away excess glue with a damp cloth.
	WALLCOVERING REMOVER A device that fits in the palm of your hand, this tool has wheels edged with a series of tiny, sharp razors for perforating paper.	When it's time to remove wallcovering, use liquid stripper and this little paper shark. Roll its sharp wheels over the wallcovering to perforate the paper. The holes will open the paper, allowing stripper or water to seep behind the wallcovering and loosen it.

FLOWER arranging supplies

	BUCKET VASES Shaped like a pail—wide at the top and narrower at the bottom— bucket vases come in many sizes and variations. Some may be made specifically as vases; others may be utilitarian objects found around the house: drinking glasses and coffee mugs with flared tops, stemware, garden pots, pitchers, crocks, galvanized buckets and pails, or classic wide-necked urns on pedestals.	For floppy flowers, you may need a device to hold the stems in place, such as floral foam, a needle-point holder (frog), crushed chicken wire, or a lattice of floral tape. To make a lattice across the mouth of the vase, fasten lengths of floral tape over the top from side to side, creating an open lattice framework. Insert flower stems between the strips of floral tape to stand them in a more upright position. Let leaves hang over the edges of the bucket to hide the edges of tape at the top of the vase.
	BUD VASES The classic bud vase with its slender, curved body has one standout feature that makes it different from all other vases: a narrow neck. Its neck and slim body limit the number of blooms it can hold. It's the top choice for the decorating pantry because it's so quick and inexpensive to fill.	A single perfect bloom standing in a tall bud vase is a star attraction on a bedside table or midnight buffet. It can stand alone as a focal point or join a band of bud vases (all with the same design) on a shelf or down the center of a dining table.

FLOWER ARRANGING SUPPLIES

WHAT TO LOOK FOR	WHAT IT IS	HOW TO USE IT
	BOWL VASES Shallow, bowl-shaped containers are a good choice for low tables where you want to see over the arrangement. Many types of vessels will serve the purpose, from soup bowls to sherbet glasses and coffee cups. Short-stemmed blossoms, such as violets, impatiens, and begonias, are best-suited for these containers.	To create a rounded arrangement, cut floral foam so that it fits inside the container and rises an inch or so above the top. Crisscross floral tape over the edges of the vase to hold the foam in place. Insert some flowers at a downward angle so they overlap the edge. To camouflage floral foam in a glass vase, line the container with moss or broad, flat foliage before inserting the water-soaked foam.
	CLASSIC VASES The urn-like shape is popular for good reason: It makes the most sense for flower arranging. The narrow neck holds the flowers in place while the wider bottom and slightly flared top allow the stems and blooms to spread out.	A classic vase is well-suited to lilies, spider mums, and other flowers with large, showy heads. When assembling an arrangement, let taller stems with tighter blossoms or buds define the upper and outer edges of the design. Place larger, showier heads near the bottom for balance.
	CYLINDRICAL VASES Straight and narrow, these slim, stately vessels make for stunning flower arrangements. Whether curved or angular, a cylinder vase has a rigid shape that's the same at the top and bottom.	Find plant material that contrasts with the rigid vertical lines of the container. Graceful grasses, curly willow, and flowering branches are good choices, as are orchids and other exotic, vine-like flowers. Or accentuate the verticality of the vase by using straight stems, such as irises, calla lilies, or cattails. Clustering cylinder vases together adds impact whether they have similar or staggered heights.
	FLORAL FOAM BLOCKS Most often called by its brand name, Oasis, floral foam is made of porous green synthetic material that holds flower stems securely in place. Some foam blocks are highly absorbent and keep your stems well-watered. Choose dry blocks for dried arrangements; buy water-absorbing blocks for wet ones.	Settle the foam into the desired vase. If the arrangement is fresh, soak the foam brick in water for several hours before beginning the arrangement. Cut flower stems to desired length and push the ends of the stems into the foam.
	FLORAL TAPE Another fastening device, this form of tape sticks to itself as it twists around a bundle of flowers. Another type actually is a strip of sticky green clay on a strip of paper, far left. Green tape hides among green leaves and stems.	Holding a bunch of stems in one hand, wrap the tape around the bundle, starting at the thicker part of the stems at the top and moving downward toward the narrower bottom. Lay the tape over itself for a round or two; then spiral it around the stems to the end.

flower arranging supplies

WHAT TO LOOK FOR	WHAT IT IS	HOW TO USE IT
	FLORIST'S FROG An old-fashioned yet timeless device for holding flower stems in place, this heavy metal disk with sharp prongs looks like an upside-down pincushion or a hedgehog.	Insert the frog at the bottom of a dry vase or container, fastening it in place with floral clay. Cut flower stems to the desired lengths and push them onto the prongs of the frog until they stand securely in place.
	PADDLE WIRE Named for the small paddle of wood that holds it, this hobbyist's wire comes in several gauges, from light to heavy. Choose a mid- to lightweight gauge for most flower-arranging and household uses. Choose between galvanized metal and green-painted wire (green is less visible in flower arrangements).	Wrap wire around bundles of dried or silk flowers or use the wire to create crafts or hobby items. For example, fasten pine cones to a grapevine wreath or wire together a bundle of evergreen branches as a door ornament for winter holidays.
	FLORIST'S PICKS AND PINS Like silk pins for fabric projects, these little fastening devices hold flower arrangements together. Some are shaped like giant hairpins; others look like green toothpicks with paddle wires attached to the ends.	Fasten floral material to foam blocks by pushing the pins over stems and branches. Push the picks into floral foam after you've wired bundles of floral material at their tops.
	FLORAL CLAY A sticky, nondrying substance with plastic qualities, this material fastens two items together. It will continue to hold while immersed in water.	Fasten pin holders, prongs, and floral foam inside flower-arranging container with small chunks of floral clay. Use it to secure the structural parts of fresh, dried, or silk floral arrangements. Apply the clay to dry objects for good adhesion.
	STONES AND MARBLES Pretty river-washed rocks in black, brown, green, and white act as anchors for a floral arrangement. Like decorative stones, marbles also weight vases and hold flower stems in place.	Fill vase with water; settle the flower stems into the water. Add stones or marbles a few at a time around the stems. Continue adding until the stems seem secure. If you use stones and marbles in glass vases, their beauty will show through and add to the look of the arrangement.

LIGHTING SUPPLIES

WHAT TO LOOK FOR	WHAT IT IS	HOW TO USE IT
	CANDLESNUFFER A safe and charming way to put out lit candles, this long-stemmed tool was used regularly before the invention of electric lights.	Lower the cup over the candle flame until the flame is extinguished.
	SPARE LIGHT BULBS Keep a variety of shapes, sizes, and wattages on hand to replace those that burn out. Soft-white bulbs provide the best light for bedrooms. Colored bulbs are fun to use to create a party mood, an intimate mood, or a rosy-cozy mood. Rooms with dark wall colors require more light than light-colored rooms. If you paint a room a darker color, you may need to change your lamps, adding more translucent lampshades or brighter bulbs to make up the difference.	Consult the fixture label for recommended wattage and follow the recommendation. Remove the lampshade or ceiling bulb cover. Unscrew the old lightbulb and screw in a replacement.
	LONG-NOSE LIGHTER Similar to a cigarette lighter except in length, this fire-lighting device passes the flame to the candlewick through a long metal stem.	For safety's sake, light candles with this flick-of-the-switch lighter instead of with matches. It's especially useful for birthday cakes with many tiny candles.
	PILLAR CANDLES Standing with the weight and dignity of columns, pillar candles vary in thickness from 2-inch to 8- and 10-inch diameters. Thicker pillars have as many as five wicks. Pillar candles are usually no more than 12 inches tall.	Arrange pillars in groups or let one stand alone as a focal point. If a pool of wax builds up and drowns the flame, pour the excess liquid wax into a metal waste container so the wick is exposed to air.
	PILLAR CANDLEHOLDERS Popular pillar candleholders resemble trays and platters. Some hold a single pillar; others hold a group of pillars with various heights.	Set a single pillar on a round dish, a small stand, or a floor-standing candleholder to make it a focal point for a room. To create a centerpiece or tabletop focal point with a number of pillars, group the pillars on a large tray or platter. Scatter pretty stones or marbles around the bases of the candles.

LIGHTING/MISCELLANEOUS SUPPLIES

WHAT TO LOOK FOR	WHAT IT IS	HOW TO USE IT
	TAPER CANDLES Narrower at the top than at the bottom, the taper candle was the first type of candle ever made.	Store tapers on their sides; standing them up in containers may cause them to warp and stick to each other. Extinguish them before they burn lower than 2 inches above the top of the candleholder. Never leave burning candles unattended.
	TAPER CANDLEHOLDERS Many different taper candleholders are available. Most are shapely stands with narrow tops into which the candles are inserted. Others have large glass bowls that fit over candle-holding bases.	Insert tapers into candleholders. If they lean or topple, remove them and use this trick: Burn another candle and drip the hot wax from its wick into the bottom of the candle-holding cup. Settle the taper into the cooling wax; then hold for a moment until the wax has solidified and the candle is stable.
	TEA LIGHTS Housed inside small cylinders, these tiny candles need no decorative holders to contain melting wax. Tea lights usually burn for six hours before their wicks extinguish in the hot wax.	Use tea lights in large numbers—in a lineup along a mantel or ledge; down the center of a table; at each place setting around a large dinner table; in a group under a grate in a fireplace.
	VOTIVE CANDLES Originally used in churches, votive candles now brighten dark corners of homes. Some are round or cylindrical; most are freestanding. However, some are poured directly into a container at the hot-wax stage of production.	Unlike tea lights, votives require a decorative holder to contain the flow of melted wax. Like tea lights, use them in groups, in line formations, or singly.
	VOTIVE CANDLEHOLDER Square, round, set in stands or stems, holders for votive candles are usually made from glass. Gather a collection to keep on hand for special occasions.	Line them in a row down the center of a table. Fill a tray with as many as it will hold. Burn a single votive as a stand-alone feature on a side table.

miscellaneous supplies

	CAN AND BOTTLE OPENER This well-known device pops tops off narrow-top bottles and lifts lids off paint and stain cans.	Push the narrow end of the opener under the lip of a can lid and press down. Slide it around to another position and press again. Eventually the lid will lift.

miscellaneous supplies

WHAT TO LOOK FOR	WHAT IT IS	HOW TO USE IT
	CLEANING SUPPLIES Keep basic cleaning supplies handy in your decorating pantry—a bucket (to contain cleaning liquids) and thirsty rags (to absorb liquids in cleanup). Car-washing cloths are one of the best buys.	Fill the bucket with water, swish in the appropriate cleanser for the job, and wipe it up with rags.
	TACK CLOTH This loosely woven fabric, impregnated with a resin, attracts every last dust particle and undesirable material on the wood surface you are about to refinish.	Unfold the fabric and wipe the surface as if you were dusting with a dust cloth. Wipe *with* the wood grain, not across it. Store the cloth in plastic to keep it from drying out.
	FURNITURE MOVERS While protecting your floors from scratches, these padded disks or sliders make moving refrigerators, sofas, tables, stoves, beds, and dressers easier. If desired, the disks can be permanently attached to furniture for frequent room arranging. They work on wood, vinyl, ceramic tile, and carpeted floors.	Match the disk or slider to the item you wish to move. If the piece of furniture doesn't have legs, use large disks at corners. Push or pull the furniture item in any direction, applying pressure low enough to avoid tilting or moving the item off the sliders.
	HEMMING TAPE A no-sew material purchased at a fabric store, this roll of white, gauze-like fabric binds two layers of fabric together when heated with a hot iron.	Lay a length of hemming tape between the two layers of fabric you want to hem, leaving none of the tape uncovered. Lay a paper towel over the fabric and press with a hot iron for about 30 seconds (check the package instructions for timing). This handy material will hem tablecloths, curtains, and small crafts projects.
	PROJECT CALCULATOR A handheld, pocket-size genius, a calculator does the math for you. The cover guides you through the steps of a decorating project. You'll find this handy item in the tool section of any home center.	Use the calculator to figure out the rug size you need for a space, the amount of tile you'll need to cover a floor, or the amount of wallcovering to purchase for an accent wall.
	SEWING KIT A travel-size sewing kit with a tiny scissors, a set of needles, a thimble, and a small selection of threads is all you need for repairs on curtains and bedding. If you sew home furnishings, you'll need a more professional kit for the decorating pantry.	Use a needle and thread to reattach curtain rings, repair a pillow cover seam, or stitch a hanging loop on the back of a decorative kitchen towel.
	STEP STOOL A two- or three-step stool folds up for easy storage.	Step up to reach high places while painting, dusting, changing a lightbulb, or arranging decorative items on high shelves.

resources

entrances

JEWEL BOX

pages 16–23

Chair: Crate and Barrel, 800/996-9960, www.crateandbarrel.com
Chest, screen, dotted pottery: Pier 1 Imports, 800/245-4595, www.pierone.com
Wall sconce, runner: IKEA Home Furnishings, 800/434-4532, www.ikea.com
Candle lamp: Target Stores, 888/304-4000, www.target.com
Console table: Cost Plus World Market, 800/267-8758, www.costplus.com
Baskets, candle stands, mirror, red bowl: antique, discontinued, or a personal belonging

TWO'S COMPANY

pages 24–25

All items: antique, discontinued, or a personal belonging

warm welcome

pages 26–27

Grass-cloth wall covering: Imperial Home Decor Group, Imperial Wall Coverings, 800/539-5399, www.ihdg.com
Mirror: Pottery Barn, 800/922-5507, www.potterybarn.com

practical magic

pages 28-29

Lamp: IKEA Home Furnishings, 800/434-4532, www.ikea.com
Laminate flooring, wainscot materials: Home Depot, www.homedepot.com

open sesame

pages 30–31

All items: antique, discontinued, or a personal belonging

LIVING rooms

VELVET ALLURE

pages 34-41

Sectional sofa: Design Within Reach, 800/944-2233, www.dwr.com
Chair, nesting tables: Crate and Barrel, 800/996-9960, www.crateandbarrel.com
Asian tables: Target Stores, 888/304-4000, www.target.com
Floor lamp, entertainment center: Pier 1 Imports, 800/245-4595, www.pierone.com
Pillows, Chinese throw, red stools, wedding baskets, velvet draperies: Cost Plus World Market, 800/267-8758
Mirror tile, wall sconce: IKEA Home Furnishings, 800/434-4532, www.ikea.com
All other items: antique, discontinued, handmade, or a personal belonging

SAND CASTLE

pages 42–43

All items: antique, discontinued, or a personal belonging

SQUARED AWAY

pages 44–45

Chair: Mitchell Gold, 800/789-5401, www.mitchellgold.com

creme fresh

pages 46-49

All items: antique, discontinued, or a personal belonging

second wind

pages 50–51

Sheepskin, large green vase: IKEA Home Furnishings, 800/434-4532, www.ikea.com
Zebra stripe pillows: Neiman Marcus, 800/825-8000, www.neimanmarcus.com
Coffee table: "Antonio Citterio" B&BItalia, USA, Inc., 800/872-1697, www.bebitalia.it

SMALL IS SAVVY

pages 54–55

Sofa: Pindler & Pindler, Inc., 805/531-9090, www.pindler.com
Columns: salvage
Ottoman: flea market
Lamp: refurbished antique
Lampshade: custom by A. W. Stavish Designs, 773/227-0117
Map: reproduction of 1784 map, Louvre Bookstore, Paris, France
All other items: personal collection

LIVING OUT BACK

pages 56–57

Decorative screen and area rug similar styles available at Pottery Barn, 800/922-5507, www.potterybarn.com

Dining chair: Pier 1 Imports, 800/245-6554, www.pierone.com

DINING ROOMS
SAFFRON SUNSHINE

pages 60-67

Wall lights, transparent curtain panels, curtain rods, baker's rack, unfinished wall-hung storage unit: IKEA Home Furnishings, 800/434-4532, www.ikea.com
Chairs: Pier 1 Imports, 800/245-4595, www.pierone.com
Tableware, lighting fixture parts: antique, discontinued, or a personal belonging

DINING LIGHT

pages 68–69

Metal table with glass top: 5-Day Furniture, 952/884-5555
Wicker chairs: Pier 1 Imports, 800/245-4595, www.pierone.com
Floral pitcher and cup: MacKenzie-Childs, 212/570-6050
Rose wineglasses: antique
Curtain panels: ABC Carpet & Home, 212/473-3000, www.abchome.com

MODERN MIX

pages 70–71

Dining room chairs: Design Within Reach, 800/944-2233, www.dwr.com

CAFE PROVENCE

pages 74–75

Dining table: Drexel, Pinehurst Collection, 952/836-2831, www.drexelheritage.com
Chandelier: Lappin Lighting, 612/339-5555

TABLE DE CHARME

pages 76–77

Table: Ballard Designs, 800/367-2810
Chairs: Crate and Barrel, 800/996-9960, www.crateandbarrel.com
Chandelier: Studio Steel Inc., 860/868-7305, www.studiosteel.com

TWO FOR TEA

pages 78–79

Chairs: Pier 1 Imports, 800/245-6554, www.pierone.com
Bi-fold doors: Home Depot, homedepot.com

GARDEN PARTY

pages 80–81

All items: antique, discontinued, or a personal belonging

KITCHENS
COFFEEHOUSE BLEND

pages 86-93

Barheight chairs, lamp, wall-hung storage, clock, mini-blinds, hardware, pot rack, canvas photographs: IKEA Home Furnishings, 800/434-4532, www.ikea.com
Kitchen towels: Target Stores, 888/304-4000, www.target.com
Laminate flooring: Home Depot, www.homedepot.com
All other items: discontinued, handmade, antique, or a personal belonging

resources

TASTE OF SWEDEN

pages 96–97

Light fixture: Lowe's Cos., Inc, 800/445-6937, www.lowes.com

Curtain fabric: Waverly, "Homestead Collection," 800/423-5881, www.waverly.com

Hardware: Amerock Corp., 800/618-9559, www.amerock.com

SLEEK & SIMPLE

pages 100–101

Countertops, faucet, backsplash tile, sink, cabinets: Home Depot, www.homedepot.com.

Glasses on shelf: Pier 1 Imports, 800/447-4371

Hanging light, cable system for curtain: IKEA Home Furnishings, 800/434-4532, www.ikea.com

Blinds: Smith + Noble, 800/765-7776

Kitchen island: Hold Everything, 800/421-2264, www.hold-everything.com

COMFORT SWEET

pages 104–105

Cabinet picture frames: Target Stores, 800/304-4000, www.target.com

Table lamp: Pariscope, 630/232-1600

Window blinds: Hunter Douglas Window Fashions, 800/937-7895, www.hunterdouglas.com

Clock: Salvation Army

BEDROOMS

LAVENDER RETREAT

pages 109-115

Floor screen: Target Stores, 800/304-4000, www.target.com

Bedside and floor lamps: Home Depot. www.homedepot.com

Wall coverings, pillow fabrics: Susan Sargeant Collection, Sherwin Williams, 800/474-3794, www.sherwinwilliams.com

Chests of drawers, quilt, pillowcases, flokati rug, chairs: IKEA Home Furnishings, 800/434-4532, www.ikea.com

All other items: antique, discontinued, or a personal belonging

SO SOOTHING

pages 116–117

Bedding: Area, New York City, 212/924-7084, www.areahome.com

Chest of drawers: Yorkshire Pine, 858/270-7463, www.yorkshirepine.com

UPSY DAISY

pages 124–125

High/low reading lamps: Pottery Barn, 800/922-5507, www.potterybarn.com

Floral and check fabrics: Laura Ashley, 800/367-2000, www.laura-ashley.com

Bedside table: Maine Cottage, 207/846-1430, www.mainecottage.com

CABLE HAVEN

pages 128–129

Cable, hardware. beadboard paneling: Home Depot, www.homedepot.com

Chair: Pier 1 Imports, 800/245-6554, www.pierone.com

All other items: antique, discontinued, or a personal belonging

BATHROOMS

SAUNA STYLE

pages 134-141

Lighting, towel bar, stones picture, towels: IKEA Home Furnishings, 800/434-4532, www.ikea.com

"Closits" stacking storage units: Sauder Woodworking, 800/523-3987, www.sauder.com

All other items: antique, discontinued, handmade, or a personal belonging

CREDITS

WATER MUSIC
pages 142–143

All items: antique, discontinued, or a personal belonging

NATURAL BEAUTY
pages 148–149

Towel: Bed, Bath & Beyond, 800/Go-Beyond, www.bedbathandbeyond.com
Moroccan table: Garnet Hill, 800/622-6216
Sisal rug: Cost Plus World Market, 800/267-8758, www.costplus.com

GREEN ROOMS
AIRY PAVILION
pages 154-161

Wicker chairs, coffee table, wrought-iron bench, folding shelf unit: Pier 1 Imports, 800/245-6554, www.pierone.com
Wicker birdcage, pillows, glass lanterns, sisal carpet: Cost Plus World Market, 800/267-8758, www.costplus.com
All other items: antique, discontinued, handmade, or a personal belonging

POTTING MIX
pages 164–165

Framed prints of pressed herbs, plant stand, pillows: Ballard Designs, 800/367-2775, www.ballarddesigns.com
Glass cloches: Exposures Home, 800/699-6993
Bamboo nesting tables, side table: antique
All other items: discontinued or a personal belonging

SUN SPACE
pages 168–169

Roman shades: "Martha Stewart Everyday," Kmart, 800/635-6278, www.bluelight.com
Ceramic pieces on shelf: antique

A SPECIAL THANKS
to those who provided materials, products, and services

SAUDER WOODWORKING, well-known manufacturer of quality ready-to-assemble furniture, supplied "Closits" modular storage system pieces, pages 134–141

ALEXANDER & ASSOCIATES, for constructing the countertop and coffee bar, pages 87, 90–93

JEFF ANDERSON, for building the dining table, pages 61, 65

SONJA CARMON, for stitching pillows and seat cushions, pages 109, 112, 114–115

DAVE DECARLO, for building the wall unit and mirror panels, pages 35–40

KIM HAYES AND ADAM JERDEE, for assembling and decorating the headboard and chests, pages 109, 112, 115

PEGGY JOHNSTON, for embellishing the dining room wall unit, pages 65–66

ADAM JERDEE, for designing the magazine ladder, pages 40–41

AMY UNDERWOOD, for research and styling assistance

DAVE UNDERWOOD, for crafting the bathroom cupboard doors, page 138

PHOTOGRAPHY
BILL HOPKINS pages 61–67, 87–93, 135–141, 174–185
GREG SCHEIDEMAN pages 17–23, 35–41, 109–115, 155–161

INDEX